FREEZER MEALS in an
Instant

65 DELICIOUS FREEZER FRIENDLY RECIPES FOR YOUR ELECTRIC PRESSURE COOKER

ERIN CHASE

ISBN 10: 1985243695
ISBN 13: 978-1985243699

Always follow safety and common-sense cooking protocol while using kitchen utensils, operating ovens or stoves, as well as electric pressure cookers, and handling uncooked food. If children are assisting in the preparation of any recipe, they should be supervised by an adult.

Instant Pot is a registered trademark of Double Insights, Inc. and the name is used in the recipe titles in this cookbook. FreezEasy is a registered trademark of FreezEasy Media.

For general information about our workshops, products and services, or to obtain technical support, please contact our Customer Care Team at support@freezeasy.com.

For more great recipes and resources, visit www.myfreezeasy.com.

FREE ONLINE WORKSHOP

Want to spend less time in the kitchen, and more time enjoying other things in life? Need dinner to "take care of itself"? Want to personalize and customize a freezer meal plan - with recipes your family will love?

MyFreezEasy will do all the heavy lifting for you! In a matter of seconds, our apps will pull together your freezer meal recipes, shopping lists, step-by-step instructions and printable labels for your meals. Load up your freezer with make-ahead meals and dinnertime will be a breeze.

In this free online workshop, you'll learn just about everything you need to know about freezer cooking and how it can transform your family's dinner experience.

Sign up for free at: www.myfreezeasy.com/workshop

TABLE OF CONTENTS

Freezer Meals Meet Instant Pot, Instant Pot Meet Freezer Meals

Freezer cooking has been a part of my life and kitchen routine for many years. It's the key "ingredient" that helps me stay "one step ahead" of these 4 hungry boys that I'm responsible for feeding everyday. And since they seem to never stop eating, I have to work to stay ahead of their bottomless pit stomachs.

Freezer meals are a great solution for having dinner planned and partly or completely prepped in advance. The best types of freezer meals are ones that can be thawed and then added straight to the oven or grill or slow cooker or Instant Pot.

Freezer Meals Meet Instant Pot, Instant Pot Meet Freezer Meals.

As the Instant Pot has taken the market by storm and invaded many homes across the world, it invaded my kitchen as well. And I quickly realized the ease and potential of using the electric pressure cooker to cook freezer meals - even from frozen solid.

This revelation and my experience in testing out the best recipes and options from "freezer to Instant Pot meals" has transformed the way that I cook and operate in the kitchen. Most nights my Instant Pot is in use, and if it's not defrosting and cooking my dinner, then it's likely steaming veggies or cooking rice or potatoes for side dishes.

Before we get to the recipes, I'd like to share some helpful tips and tricks for using the Instant Pot to prepare your frozen meals.

Instant Pot Freezer Meals 101

The electric pressure cooker, commonly known as the Instant Pot, is a magical small kitchen appliance that helps cut the dinner prep time in half - sometimes more, depending on the recipe.

When you combine the make ahead meals concept of freezer cooking with the ease and speed of the Instant Pot, what you end up with is the busy mom's cooking dream team. With a few meals prepped and into the freezer, you then can drop them frozen into the Instant Pot with some water or stock, and you end up wanting to hug and kiss your Instant Pot (not that I've done that, or anything.)

Before we get to the delicious recipes in this cookbook, we need to go over how to freeze your meal, how to get your frozen meal into your electric pressure cooker, and then of course how to get it to the table.

The first and most important tip is to freeze your meal in a round bowl that is slightly smaller in diameter than the insert of your Instant Pot. This will allow your freezer meal to freeze into round shape that will easily fit into the insert. Because you can't fit a rectangular meal into a round dish, it's important to freeze it in a way that will fit without issue.

Simply take a round-ish or even square-ish plastic container, and try to nest it into your insert. If it fits, then use it to make and shape your freezer meal.

Place the bowl on the counter and then add a plastic freezer baggie into the bowl and open up the top of the bag to add the ingredients. Let the ingredients in the baggie take the shape of the bowl, so the bag rounds out. Put the bowl and the freezer baggie with the meal into the freezer together. When frozen solid, take the bowl out of the freezer and set it on the counter to return to room temperature and then you can use it for other things.

Your meal is now frozen into a big round ball, or rather the "ball of deliciousness," as I like to call it.

When it's time to cook your Freezer to Instant Pot meal, you can take out the baggie with the ball of delicious and place it into a bowl with warm water. Leave it in the water for about 5 minutes, or long enough to get the baggie and the frozen ingredients to separate from each other. All you need is the food to separate from the bag so that you can transfer the food into the Instant Pot insert.

You can just flip the bag upside and add the frozen ball of delicious right into the insert. You'll want to add a cup of water or stock in with the meal so that the pressure cooker reads the liquid and begins the pressurization process properly.

Once the frozen meal and liquid are in the insert, you can turn it on and pressure cook as directed. (Please note that the cooking times vary slightly for cooking from fresh and cooking from frozen. All of the recipes below indicate time adjustments for cooking from frozen.)

As the appliance comes to full pressure, it will thaw the frozen ball of delicious and then pressure cook as you've directed it to with the cooking function and cycle. Note that the pressure build time will take longer if you are cooking from frozen, than if you are cooking with a fresh-made meal. For example, it takes about 8 to 10 minutes for a simple chili recipe to come to pressure when making fresh. It can take upwards of 20 to 25 minutes to come to pressure when it starts frozen. This is important to know for timing and planning your dinner schedule.

From prep to freezing in a round bowl, to quick-thawing and adding the meal plus liquid to the insert, this really is a fantastic hands-off way to get a meal from the freezer on to the table in less than an hour.

The best types of freezer to Instant Pot meals are ground beef-based chili, chicken to slice or shred, soups and stews, plus pork or beef roasts with sauce.

If you are making a pot roast with vegetables, you will need to pressure cook the roast with sauce by itself for for 30-50 minutes, and then add your vegetables and cook it all together for 1-5 more minutes. Because of the dual cooking times for a meal like this, I recommend one of two things:

1. Freeze the veggies in a smaller quart sized bag and either wrap it up and put it in with the roast or tape the bags together so you know those two, the veggies and roast go together.Then you cook the roast from frozen, then add the veggies from frozen and then cook it as recommended in the recipe.
2. Put the vegetables and roast together in the freezer meal bag. You can put it all together into the bag, but then only add the beef roast and sauce to the Instant Pot and cook the roast and sauce first. You can keep the potatoes in the freezer meal bag in the fridge and cook them at the end with the roast.

Let's talk through the time breakdown and step-by-step for making a ground beef-based chili. It is literally like 2 minutes of hands on time, and it will be bubbling and ready to ladle into bowls in less than an hour.

You freeze the chili in a round bowl. On cooking day, you take the frozen solid ball of chili and add it to a bowl of warm water for 5 minutes to loosen it from the bag. Add 1 cup of water or beef stock to the insert and then add the frozen chili. Press the Beans and Chili cooking function, or High Pressure for 30 minutes. Put the lid on, set the valve to sealing and let the Instant Pot take it from there. It will take about 20 minutes to come to pressure and 30 minutes to cook. You can quick release the pressure and your bubbling chili is waiting to be served.

- Thaw to remove from bag - 5 minutes
- Pressure build with frozen chili - 20 minutes
- Pressure cook time set - 30 minutes
- Quick release - 1 minute

And in less than an hour, your chili is on your dinner table. With just 2 minutes of hands on time. You'll be freed up to help with homework, make phone calls, reschedule appointments, look for lost soccer cleats, pack lunches for the next day, or whatever else you might be doing in and around your kitchen in the afternoon-evening hours.

Understanding Our Recipes

Now that we understand how freezer meals work from prep to freeze to cook to serve, let's take a moment to learn how the recipes in this cookbook are formatted.

First, any necessary water is listed with the ingredients. Not all recipes have water, but they will have another liquid like stock or sauce that takes the place of the water. The other ingredients that are being pressure cooked are listed, and there might be an ingredient or two in a few recipes that is mixed in at the end of the cooking cycle. Also, each recipe includes some suggested side dishes and garnishes.

With the ground beef based recipes, we have both cooking directions for browning the ground beef in a skillet, as well as browning the ground beef on Saute mode of your Instant Pot. Many times that I'm making a set of freezer meals, I will "batch brown" the ground beef in 4 to 10 lb. batches. For so many of our freezer meals, the ground beef is already browned. But the option to use the Saute function is there if you are making the meal fresh.

The directions typically include what to add and when to the insert, as well as how to set the valve (all Sealing for the recipes in this book.) Then it lists the pressure cooking instructions, followed by the recommended pressure release instructions. For example,

Set to Sealing.
Cook: Manual, High for 15 minutes.
Release: Natural or Quick.

So here you can see mixing all the ingredients with the water, here is the instruction on how the valve should be, or the release vale or steam valve sealing, the pressure cooking instructions for this recipe, manual high pressure for 15 minutes. And then we will give you the release instructions so in this case you can get do natural or quick.

The recipes are all written for 4 servings sizes. If you increase the number of servings and the ingredient quantity, you might need to adjust the pressure cooking time by a few minutes. You won't need to "double the time" if you are "doubling the ingredients." That is not how an electric pressure cooker works. If you have twice the food, you might just need to increase the cook time slightly. Consult your appliance user guide for your particular manufacturer on any adjustments like that that need to be made.

And with that, let's get to the recipes!

Instant Pot 5-Ingredient Chili

Yield:	4 servings
Prep Time:	10 minutes
Cook Time:	15 minutes plus pressure build and release time

Ingredients

- 1 lb. ground beef
- 1 small white onion
- 2 - 15 oz. cans red kidney beans
- 2 - 15 oz. diced tomatoes & green chiles
- 2 Tbsp chili powder
- Salt and pepper
- Garnish: shredded cheese
- 1 cup hot water
- Side: salad
- 1 gallon-size freezer baggie

Prepare to Freeze Instructions

1. Brown ground beef.
2. Open and drain red kidney beans.
3. Open diced tomatoes with green chiles.
- To gallon-size plastic freezer baggie in a round bowl/dish, add the following ingredients:
  - Browned ground beef
  - Drained red kidney beans
  - Diced tomatoes with green chiles
  - Diced onion
  - 2 Tbsp chili powder
  - Salt and pepper
  - Do NOT add water before freezing, add that at time of pressure cooking
- Remove as much air as possible and seal. Add label to baggie and freeze.

Cooking Directions

1. Dice the onion.
2. Open and drain the 2 cans of red kidney beans. Open 2 cans diced tomatoes with green chiles.
3. In a large skillet, brown the ground beef with the onion and some salt and pepper. Drain and add the browned ground beef to the pressure cooker insert.
4. Note: You can skip the skillet and brown the ground beef using the Saute Mode of your Instant Pot. Tap on Saute, adjust to More/High, and brown the ground beef with the diced onion. Drain, if needed, and return the browned ground beef to the insert.
5. Mix in the diced tomatoes with green chiles, drained red kidney beans, chili powder and hot water into the electric pressure cooker insert.
6. Steam valve: Sealing.
7. Pressure Cook: Manual/High for 15 minutes.
8. Release: Natural or Quick.
9. Prepare the salad.
10. Serve Instant Pot 5-Ingredient Chili with shredded cheese garnish and salad.

Freeze, Thaw & Pressure Cook Instructions

Put baggie in the freezer and freeze up to 6 months in fridge freezer or 12 months in a deep freezer. Thaw in the fridge overnight, or a bowl of warm water for about 20 minutes, before transferring to pressure cooker insert with hot water and pressure cooking as directed.

If cooking freezer meal from partially thawed, add the hot water to the insert, add the frozen ingredients and adjust Pressure Cook time to 30 minutes.

Instant Pot Asian Shredded Beef

Yield:	4 servings
Prep Time:	10 minutes
Cook Time:	45 minutes plus pressure build and release time

Ingredients

- 2 lbs. beef chuck roast
- 1/2 cup hot water
- Salt and pepper
- 1/3 cup hoisin sauce
- 1/3 cup soy sauce
- 2 Tbsp rice vinegar
- 2 Tbsp honey
- 1 Tbsp sesame oil
- 1 tsp ground ginger
- 1 tsp crushed red pepper
- Garnish: sliced green onions
- Side: rice
- Side: veggies
- 1 gallon-size freezer baggie

Prepare to Freeze Instructions

- In a mixing bowl, whisk together hoisin sauce, soy sauce, rice vinegar, honey, sesame oil, ground ginger and crushed red pepper.
- To gallon-size plastic freezer baggie in a round bowl/dish, add the following ingredients:
  - Beef chuck roast
  - Salt and pepper
  - Prepared sauce
  - Do NOT add water to the freezer meal bag, add that at time of pressure cooking
- Remove as much air as possible and seal. Add label to baggie and freeze.

Cooking Directions

1. Place the beef roast into the base of the electric pressure cooker insert with the hot water and season with salt and pepper.
2. In a mixing bowl, whisk together the hoisin sauce, soy sauce, rice vinegar, honey, sesame oil, ginger and crushed red pepper.
3. Pour the sauce over the beef in the electric pressure cooker insert.
4. Steam value: Sealing.
5. Cook on: Manual/High for 45 minutes.
6. Release: Natural or Quick.
7. Once finished cooking, shred the beef with 2 forks and mix into the sauce.
8. Cook the rice, as directed.
9. Prepare the veggies.
10. Serve Instant Pot Asian Shredded Beef over rice with veggies and green onion garnish.

Freeze, Thaw & Pressure Cook Instructions

Put baggie in the freezer and freeze up to 6 months in fridge freezer or 12 months in a deep freezer. Thaw in the fridge overnight, or a bowl of warm water for about 20 minutes, before transferring to pressure cooker insert with hot water. Pressure cook as directed.

If cooking freezer meal from partially thawed, add the hot water to the insert, add the frozen ingredients and adjust Pressure Cook time to 75 minutes.

Instant Pot Bacon Cheeseburger Chili

Yield:	4 servings
Prep Time:	15 minutes
Cook Time:	15 minutes plus pressure build and release time

Ingredients

- 1 lb. ground beef
- 1/2 cup hot water
- 1 Tbsp minced onion
- 1 tsp garlic powder
- 2 - 15 oz. cans white beans
- 2 cups beef broth
- 2 cups shredded cheddar cheese
- 2 cups whole milk
- Salt and pepper
- Garnish: crumbled strips bacon
- Side: veggies
- 1 gallon-size freezer baggie

Prepare to Freeze Instructions

- Brown ground beef with minced onion and garlic powder. Set aside to cool.
- Open, drain and rinse 2 cans of white beans.
- To gallon-size plastic freezer baggie in a round bowl/dish, add the following ingredients:
  - Browned ground beef
  - Canned white beans
  - Salt and pepper
  - Do NOT add beef broth to the freezer meal bag, add that at time of pressure cooking
- Remove as much air as possible and seal. Add label to baggie and freeze.

Cooking Directions

1. Open, drain, and rinse the 2 cans of white beans.
2. In a large saucepan, brown the ground beef with the minced onion and garlic powder. Drain and add the browned ground beef to the pressure cooker insert.
3. Note: You can skip the skillet and brown the ground beef using the Saute Mode of your Instant Pot. Tap on Saute, adjust to More/High, and brown the ground beef with the minced onion and garlic powder. Drain, if needed, and return the browned ground beef to the insert.
4. Stir in the drained white beans, and beef broth with the hot water.
5. Steam valve: Sealing.
6. Cook on: Manual/High for 15 minutes.
7. Release: Natural or Quick.
8. Stir in the whole milk and only half of the shredded cheese to the cooked chili. Use remaining shredded cheese for garnish.
9. Cook and crumble the bacon, if needed.
10. Prepare veggies.
11. Serve Instant Pot Bacon Cheeseburger Chili with bacon and shredded cheese garnish, and veggies.

Freeze, Thaw & Pressure Cook Instructions

Put baggie in the freezer and freeze up to 6 months in fridge freezer or 12 months in a deep freezer. Thaw in the fridge overnight, or a bowl of warm water for about 20 minutes, before transferring to pressure cooker insert with 2 cups beef broth. Pressure cook as directed. (Stir in whole milk and shredded cheese about 10 minutes before serving.)

If cooking freezer meal from partially thawed, add the hot water to the insert, add the frozen ingredients and adjust Pressure Cook time to 30 to 35 minutes.

Instant Pot Baja Shredded Chicken Tacos

Yield: 4 servings
Prep Time: 10 minutes
Cook Time: 15 minutes plus pressure build and release time

Ingredients

- 2 large boneless chicken breasts
- 4 boneless chicken thighs
- 1/2 cup hot water
- 1/2 cup brown sugar
- 1 Tbsp cumin
- 1/2 cup salsa
- 4 oz. can green chiles
- Salt and pepper
- 8 flour tortillas
- Side: salad
- 1 gallon-size freezer baggie

Prepare to Freeze Instructions

- Open can of green chiles.
- To gallon-size plastic freezer baggie in a round bowl/dish, add the following ingredients:
  - Chicken breasts
  - Chicken thighs
  - 1/2 cup brown sugar
  - 1 Tbsp cuminfroz
  - Canned green chiles
  - Salt and pepper
  - Do NOT add water to the freezer meal bag, add that at time of pressure cooking
- Remove as much air as possible and seal. Add label to baggie and freeze.

Cooking Directions

1. Place the chicken breasts and chicken thighs into the electric pressure cooker insert with the hot water. Add the brown sugar, ground cumin, salsa, green chilies, salt and pepper into the electric pressure cooking insert.
2. Steam valve: Sealing.
3. Cook on: Manual/High for 15 minutes.
4. Release: Natural or Quick.
5. Once finished cooking, shred the chicken with 2 forks and mix into the sauce.
6. Spoon the shredded chicken into tortillas and make tacos.
7. Prepare the salad.
8. Serve Instant Pot Baja Shredded Chicken Tacos with side salad.

Freeze, Thaw & Pressure Cook Instructions

Put baggie in the freezer and freeze up to 6 months in fridge freezer or 12 months in a deep freezer. Thaw in the fridge overnight, or a bowl of warm water for about 20 minutes, before adding contents of bag plus water to electric pressure cooker insert. Pressure cook as directed.

If cooking freezer meal from partially thawed, add the hot water to the insert, add the frozen ingredients and adjust Pressure Cook time to 23 to 25 minutes.

Instant Pot Balsamic & Brown Sugar Pulled Pork

Yield: 4 servings
Prep Time: 5 minutes
Cook Time: 40 minutes plus pressure build and release time

Ingredients

- 2 lbs. pork roast
- 1 cup hot water
- Salt and pepper
- 1/4 cup brown sugar
- 2 Tbsp minced onion
- 1 tsp garlic powder
- 1/4 cup balsamic vinegar
- Side: fruit
- Side: potato chips
- 1 gallon-size freezer baggie

Prepare to Freeze Instructions

- To gallon-size plastic freezer baggie in a round bowl/dish, add the following ingredients:
  - Pork roast
  - Salt and pepper
  - 1/4 cup brown sugar
  - 2 Tbsp minced onion
  - 1 tsp garlic powder
  - 1/4 cup balsamic vinegar
  - Do NOT add water to the freezer meal bag, add that at time of pressure cooking
- Remove as much air as possible and seal. Add label to baggie and freeze.

Cooking Directions

1. In a small bowl, whisk together the brown sugar, minced onion, garlic powder and balsamic vinegar.
2. Place the pork roast into the electric pressure cooker insert with the hot water. and season with salt and pepper. Pour the sauce on and around the pork.
3. Steam valve: Sealing.
4. Cook on: Manual/High for 40 minutes.
5. Release: Natural or Quick.
6. Once finished cooking, shred the pork with 2 forks and mix into the sauce. Strain before serving.
7. Prepare fruit.
8. Serve Instant Pot Balsamic & Brown Sugar Pulled Pork with chips and fruit.

Freeze, Thaw & Pressure Cook Instructions

Put baggie in the freezer and freeze up to 6 months in fridge freezer or 12 months in a deep freezer. Thaw in the fridge overnight, or a bowl of warm water for about 20 minutes, before adding contents of bag plus water to electric pressure cooker insert. Pressure cook as directed.

If cooking freezer meal from partially thawed, add the hot water to the insert, add the frozen ingredients and adjust Pressure Cook time to 65 minutes.

Instant Pot Beef & Black Bean Chili

Yield: 4 servings
Prep Time: 15 minutes
Cook Time: 15 minutes plus pressure build and release time

Ingredients

- 1 lb. ground beef
- 1 Tbsp minced onion
- 1 tsp garlic powder
- 2 - 15 oz. cans black beans
- 2 - 15 oz. cans tomato sauce
- 2 Tbsp chili powder
- Salt and pepper
- 1 cup hot water
- Garnish: shredded cheddar cheese
- Garnish: sour cream
- Side: veggies
- 1 gallon-size freezer baggie

Prepare to Freeze Instructions

- Brown ground beef with the minced onion and garlic powder.
- Open, drain and rinse cans of black beans.
- Open cans of tomato sauce.
- To gallon-size plastic freezer baggie in a round bowl/dish, add the following ingredients:
  - Browned and cooled ground beef
  - Black beans, drained and rinsed
  - Tomato sauce
  - 2 Tbsp chili powder
  - Salt and pepper to taste
  - Do NOT add water to the freezer meal bag, add that at time of pressure cooking
- Remove as much air as possible and seal. Add label and freeze.

Cooking Directions

1. Open, drain and rinse the black beans. Open the cans of tomato sauce.
2. In a large skillet, brown the ground beef with the minced onion and garlic powder. Drain and add the browned ground beef to the pressure cooker insert.
3. Note: You can skip the skillet and brown the ground beef using the Saute Mode of your Instant Pot. Tap on Saute, adjust to More/High, and brown the ground beef with the minced onion and garlic powder. Drain, if needed, and return the browned ground beef to the insert.
4. Stir in the black beans, tomato sauce, chili powder, salt and pepper with the hot water into the electric pressure cooker insert.
5. Steam valve: Sealing.
6. Cook on: Manual/High for 15 minutes.
7. Release: Natural or Quick.
8. Prepare veggies.
9. Serve Instant Pot Beef & Black Bean Chili with optional garnishes and veggies.

Freeze, Thaw & Pressure Cook Instructions

Put baggie in the freezer and freeze up to 6 months in fridge freezer or 12 months in a deep freezer. Thaw in the fridge overnight, or a bowl of warm water for about 20 minutes, before transferring to pressure cooker insert with hot water and pressure cooking.

If cooking freezer meal from partially thawed, add the hot water to the insert, add the frozen ingredients and adjust Pressure Cook time to 30 to 35 minutes.

Instant Pot Beef & Sweet Potato Stew

Yield: 4 servings
Prep Time: 15 minutes
Cook Time: 20 minutes plus pressure build and release time

Ingredients

- 1 Tbsp olive oil
- 1 lb. stew beef
- 1/2 cup hot water
- 4 small sweet potatoes
- 4 whole carrots
- 2 celery stalks
- 1 small white onion
- 4 cup beef broth
- 6 oz. can tomato paste
- 1 tsp paprika
- 1 tsp dried thyme
- Salt and pepper
- Side: salad
- 1 gallon-size freezer baggie

Prepare to Freeze Instructions

- Peel and dice sweet potatoes. Peel and dice carrots.
- Chop celery stalks. Chop onion.
- Open can of tomato paste.
- To gallon-size plastic freezer baggie in a round bowl/dish, add the following ingredients:
  - Stew beef
  - Diced sweet potatoes
  - Diced carrots
  - Chopped celery
  - Chopped onion
  - Beef broth
  - Tomato paste
  - 1 tsp paprika
  - 1 tsp dried thyme
  - Do NOT add water to the freezer meal bag, add that at time of pressure cooking
- Remove as much air as possible and seal. Add label to baggie and freeze.

Cooking Directions

1. Open can of tomato paste.
2. Peel and dice the sweet potatoes. Peel and dice the carrots.
3. Chop the celery. Chop the onion.
4. Place the stew beef pieces into the pressure cooker insert with the hot water. Stir in the chopped celery, onion, sweet potatoes and carrots. Stir in the beef broth and tomato paste. Whisk in the paprika and dried thyme.
5. Steam valve: Sealing.
6. Cook on: Manual/High for 20 minutes.
7. Release: Natural or Quick.
8. Prepare the salad.
9. Serve Instant Pot Beef & Sweet Potato Stew with salad.

Freeze, Thaw & Pressure Cook Instructions

Put baggie in the freezer and freeze up to 6 months in fridge freezer or 12 months in a deep freezer. Thaw in the fridge overnight, or a bowl of warm water for about 20 minutes, before adding contents of bag plus water to electric pressure cooker insert. Pressure cook as directed.

If cooking freezer meal from partially thawed, add the hot water to the insert, add the frozen ingredients and adjust Pressure Cook time to 30 to 35 minutes.

Instant Pot Beef and Vegetable Soup

Yield:	4 servings
Prep Time:	15 minutes
Cook Time:	25 minutes plus pressure build and release time

Ingredients

- 1 lb. ground beef
- 15 oz. can black beans
- 15 oz. can diced tomatoes
- 3 cups frozen mixed vegetables
- 1 Tbsp Italian seasoning
- 1 tsp garlic powder
- 3 cups chicken broth
- Salt and pepper
- 1 cup hot water
- Side: dinner rolls
- 1 gallon-size freezer baggie

Freezeasy Meal Prep Directions

- Brown and drain ground beef.
- Open, drain and rinse black beans.
- Open diced tomatoes.
- To gallon-size plastic freezer baggie in a round bowl/dish, add the following ingredients:
  - Ground beef, browned and cooled
  - Black beans, drained and rinsed
  - Diced tomatoes, undrained
  - Frozen mixed vegetables
  - 1 Tbsp Italian seasoning
  - 1 tsp garlic powder
  - Salt and pepper
  - Do NOT add chicken broth or water to the freezer meal bag, add that at time of pressure cooking.
- Remove as much air as possible and seal. Add label to baggie and freeze.

Cooking Directions

1. Open, drain and rinse the black beans. Open the can of diced tomatoes.
2. Brown and drain the ground beef. Add the browned ground beef to the pressure cooker insert.
3. Note: You can skip the skillet and brown the ground beef using the Saute Mode of your Instant Pot. Tap on Saute, adjust to More/High, and brown the ground beef. Drain, if needed, and return the browned ground beef to the insert.
4. Stir in the black beans, diced tomatoes, frozen mixed vegetables, Italian seasoning, garlic powder, and chicken broth with the hot water into the electric pressure cooker insert.
5. Steam valve: Sealing.
6. Cook on: Manual/High for 25 minutes.
7. Release: Natural or Quick.
8. Warm dinner rolls.
9. Serve Instant Pot Beef and Vegetable Soup with dinner rolls.

Freeze, Thaw & Pressure Cook Instructions

Put baggie in the freezer and freeze up to 6 months in fridge freezer or 12 months in a deep freezer. Thaw in the fridge overnight, or a bowl of warm water for about 20 minutes, before transferring to pressure cooker insert with 3 cups chicken broth.

If cooking freezer meal from partially thawed, add the broth or hot water plus equivalent bullion to the insert, add the frozen ingredients and adjust Pressure Cook time to 30 to 35 minutes.

Instant Pot Beef Chili with Refried Beans

Yield: 4 servings
Prep Time: 15 minutes
Cook Time: 15 minutes plus pressure build and release time

Ingredients

- 1 lb. ground beef
- 1 Tbsp minced onion
- 1 tsp garlic powder
- 15 oz. can diced tomatoes
- 15 oz. can refried beans
- 1 Tbsp chili powder
- 1 tsp ground cumin
- 2 cups beef broth
- Salt and pepper
- Side: cornbread
- 1 gallon-size freezer baggie

Prepare to Freeze Instructions

- Brown ground beef with minced onion and garlic powder. Let cool.
- Open and drain can of diced tomatoes. Open can of refried beans.
- To gallon-size plastic freezer baggie in a round bowl/dish, add the following ingredients:
  - Browned ground beef
  - Diced tomatoes
  - Refried beans
  - 1 Tbsp chili powder
  - 1 tsp ground cumin
  - Salt and pepper
  - Do NOT add broth or water to the freezer meal bag, add that at time of pressure cooking.
- Remove as much air as possible and seal. Add label to baggie and freeze.

Cooking Directions

1. Open and drain the diced tomatoes.
2. Open the refried beans.
3. In a large skillet, brown the ground beef with the minced onion and garlic powder. Drain and add the browned ground beef to the electric pressure cooker insert.
4. Note: You can skip the skillet and brown the ground beef using the Saute Mode of your Instant Pot. Tap on Saute, adjust to More/High, and brown the ground beef with the minced onion and garlic powder. Drain, if needed, and return the browned ground beef to the insert.
5. Stir in the diced tomatoes, refried beans, chili powder, ground cumin, beef broth and hot water. Season with salt and pepper to taste.
6. Steam valve: Sealing.
7. Cook on: Manual/High for 15 minutes. Release: Natural or Quick.
8. Prepare the cornbread, as directed.
9. Serve Instant Pot Beef Chili with Refried Beans with cornbread.

Freeze, Thaw & Pressure Cook Instructions

Put baggie in the freezer and freeze up to 6 months in fridge freezer or 12 months in a deep freezer. Thaw in the fridge overnight, or a bowl of warm water for about 20 minutes, before transferring to pressure cooker insert with 2 cups beef broth. Pressure cook as directed.

If cooking freezer meal from partially thawed, add the broth or hot water plus equivalent bullion to the insert, add the frozen ingredients and adjust Pressure Cook time to 30 to 35 minutes.

Instant Pot Bolognese Sauce

Yield: 4 servings
Prep Time: 10 minutes
Cook Time: 15 minutes plus pressure build and release time

Ingredients

- 4 slices bacon
- 1 lb. ground beef
- 1 Tbsp minced onion
- 1 tsp garlic powder
- 28 oz. can crushed tomatoes
- 1 Tbsp Italian seasoning
- 4 whole carrots
- 1 celery stalk
- 1/2 small white onion
- 1 cup hot water
- Garnish: grated Parmesan cheese
- Side: pasta
- Side: veggies
- 1 gallon-size freezer baggie

Prepare to Freeze Instructions

- Cook and crumble bacon.
- Brown ground beef with minced onion and garlic powder. Let cool.
- Peel and shred carrots. Finely chop celery stalk and onion.
- To gallon-size plastic freezer baggie in a round bowl/dish, add the following ingredients:
  - Browned ground beef
  - Crushed tomatoes
  - Italian seasoning
  - Shredded carrots
  - Chopped celery
  - Chopped onion
  - Cooked and crumbled bacon
  - Do NOT add water to the freezer meal bag, add that at time of pressure cooking
- Remove as much air as possible and seal. Add label to baggie and freeze.

Cooking Directions

1. Cook and crumble the bacon.
2. Shred the carrots. Finely chop the celery and onion.
3. In a large saucepan, brown the ground beef with the minced onion and garlic powder. Drain and add the browned ground beef to the pressure cooker insert.
4. Note: You can skip the skillet and brown the ground beef using the Saute Mode of your Instant Pot. Tap on Saute, adjust to More/High, and brown the ground beef with the minced onion and garlic powder. Drain, if needed, and return the browned ground beef to the insert.
5. Stir in the crushed tomatoes, Italian seasoning, shredded carrots, chopped celery, chopped onion, crumbled bacon and hot water into the electric pressure cooker insert.
6. Steam valve: Sealing.
7. Cook on: Manual/High for 15 minutes.
8. Release: Natural or Quick.
9. Cook the pasta, as directed.
10. Prepare veggies.

Freeze, Thaw & Pressure Cook Instructions

Put baggie in the freezer and freeze up to 6 months in fridge freezer or 12 months in a deep freezer. Thaw in the fridge overnight, or a bowl of warm water for about 20 minutes, before transferring to pressure cooker insert with 1 cup hot water.

If cooking freezer meal from partially thawed, add the hot water to the insert, add the frozen ingredients and adjust Pressure Cook time to 30 to 35 minutes.

Instant Pot Borracho Shredded Chicken

Yield: 4 servings
Prep Time: 15 minutes
Cook Time: 15 minutes plus pressure build and release time

Ingredients

- 2 large boneless chicken breasts
- 4 boneless chicken thighs
- 1/2 cup hot water
- Salt and pepper
- 1 small white onion
- 1 tsp minced garlic
- 1/2 tsp oregano
- 1 cup beer
- 12 flour tortillas
- Garnish: pico de gallo
- Garnish: sour cream
- Side: salad
- 1 gallon-size freezer baggie

Prepare to Freeze Instructions

- Slice onions.
- To gallon-size plastic freezer baggie in a round bowl/dish, add the following ingredients:
  - Chicken breasts
  - Chicken thighs
  - Salt and pepper
  - Sliced onion
  - Minced garlic
  - 1/2 tsp oregano
  - 1 cup beer
  - Do NOT add water to the freezer meal bag, add that at time of pressure cooking
- Remove as much air as possible and seal. Add label to baggie and freeze.

Cooking Directions

1. Slice the white onion.
2. Place the chicken breasts and chicken thighs into the electric pressure cooker insert with the hot water. Add the sliced onion, minced garlic, oregano, salt and pepper around the chicken. Pour the beer over the top.
3. Steam valve: Sealing.
4. Cook on: Manual/High for 15 minutes.
5. Release: Natural or Quick.
6. Once finished cooking, shred the chicken with 2 forks and mix into the sauce. Spoon the shredded chicken into tortillas and make tacos. Add favorite taco toppings as garnish.
7. Prepare the salad.
8. Serve Instant Pot Borracho Shredded Chicken as tacos with salad.

Freeze, Thaw & Pressure Cook Instructions

Put baggie in the freezer and freeze up to 6 months in fridge freezer or 12 months in a deep freezer. Thaw in the fridge overnight, or a bowl of warm water for about 20 minutes, before adding contents of bag plus water to electric pressure cooker insert. Pressure cook as directed.

If cooking freezer meal from partially thawed, add the hot water to the insert, add the frozen ingredients and adjust Pressure Cook time to 23 to 25 minutes.

Instant Pot Butter Chicken

Yield:	4 servings
Prep Time:	10 minutes
Cook Time:	15 minutes plus pressure build and release time

Ingredients

- 2 large boneless chicken breasts
- 4 boneless chicken thighs
- 1/2 cup hot water
- 1/4 cup butter
- 1 small white onion
- 8 oz. can tomato sauce
- 2 tsp minced garlic
- 1 Tbsp garam masala
- 1 cup chicken stock
- Salt and pepper
- 1 cup heavy cream
- Side: pita bread
- Side: salad
- 1 gallon-size freezer baggie

Prepare to Freeze Instructions

- Dice onion.
- Open can of tomato sauce.
- To gallon-size plastic freezer baggie in a round bowl/dish, add the following ingredients:
  - Chicken breasts
  - Chicken thighs
  - 1/4 cup butter
  - Diced onion
  - Tomato sauce
  - 2 tsp minced garlic
  - 1 Tbsp garam masala
  - Salt and pepper
  - Do NOT add chicken stock to the freezer meal bag, add that at time of pressure
  - cooking
- Remove as much air as possible and seal. Add label to baggie and freeze.

Cooking Directions

1. Dice the onion.
2. Place the chicken breasts and chicken thighs into the electric pressure cooker insert with the hot water. Add the butter, diced white onions, tomato sauce, minced garlic, garam masala, chicken stock, salt and pepper on top of the chicken.
3. Steam valve: Sealing.
4. Cook on: Manual/High for 15 minutes.
5. Release: Natural or Quick.
6. After you open the lid, stir in the heavy cream into the tomato sauce in the insert and keep on warm setting for 5 minutes to heat through.
7. Once finished cooking, gently shred the chicken with 2 forks and mix into the sauce.
8. Prepare the salad.
9. Serve Instant Pot Butter Chicken with pita bread and salad.

Freeze, Thaw & Pressure Cook Instructions

Put baggie in the freezer and freeze up to 6 months in fridge freezer or 12 months in a deep freezer. Thaw in the fridge overnight, or a bowl of warm water for about 20 minutes, before adding contents of bag plus 1/2 cup hot water and 1 cup chicken stock to electric pressure cooker insert. Pressure cook as directed. After cooking, stir in heavy cream and keep on warm setting for 5 minutes to warm through.

If cooking freezer meal from partially thawed, add the hot water and chicken stock to the insert, add the frozen ingredients and adjust Pressure Cook time to 23 to 25 minutes.

Instant Pot Cheesy Garlic Pork Chops

Yield:	4 servings
Prep Time:	5 minutes
Cook Time:	20 minutes plus pressure build and release time

Ingredients

- 4 boneless pork chops
- 1/2 cup hot water
- Salt and pepper
- 2 Tbsp melted butter
- 2 tsp minced garlic
- 1 tsp onion powder
- 1 cup shredded mild cheddar cheese
- Side: dinner rolls
- Side: veggies
- 1 gallon-size freezer baggie

Prepare to Freeze Instructions

- In a small bowl, stir melted butter, minced garlic, and onion powder.
- To gallon-size plastic freezer baggie in a round bowl/dish, add the following ingredients:
  - Boneless pork chops
  - Melted butter mixture, brushed onto each pork chop
  - Do NOT add water to the freezer meal bag, add that at time of pressure cooking
- Remove as much air as possible and seal. Add label to baggie and freeze.

Cooking Directions

1. Place the pork chops into the electric pressure cooker insert and season with salt and pepper. Add the hot water.
2. In a small bowl, stir the melted butter, minced garlic, and onion powder. Brush it onto the pork chops.
3. Steam Valve: Sealing
4. Cook on: Manual/High for 20 minutes.
5. Release: Natural or Quick.
6. Once lid is opened, leave on warm and add a few pinchfulls of shredded mild cheddar cheese onto each pork chop. Let sit for 3 to 5 minutes for cheese to melt.
7. Prepare veggies.
8. Warm the dinner rolls.
9. Serve Instant Pot Cheesy Garlic Pork Chops with veggies and dinner rolls. Serve Instant Pot Borracho Shredded Chicken as tacos with salad.

Freeze, Thaw & Pressure Cook Instructions

Put baggie in the freezer and freeze up to 6 months in fridge freezer or 12 months in a deep freezer. Thaw in the fridge overnight, or a bowl of warm water for about 20 minutes, before transferring to pressure cooker insert with hot water. Pressure cook as directed and top with shredded cheese after cooking.

If cooking freezer meal from partially thawed, add the hot water to the insert, add the frozen ingredients and adjust Pressure Cook time to 24 minutes.

Instant Pot Chicken & Black Bean Taco Salad

Yield:	4 servings
Prep Time:	10 minutes
Cook Time:	15 minutes plus pressure build and release time

Ingredients

- 4 small boneless chicken breasts
- 1/2 cup hot water
- 15 oz. can black beans
- 1 cup red salsa
- 1 packet taco seasoning
- Salt and pepper
- Garnish: guacamole
- Side: shredded lettuce
- Side: veggies
- 1 gallon-size freezer baggie

Prepare to Freeze Instructions

- Open, drain and rinse can of black beans.
- To gallon-size plastic freezer baggie in a round bowl/dish, add the following ingredients:
  - Chicken breasts
  - Black beans
  - 1 cup red salsa
  - 1 packet taco seasoning
  - Salt and pepper
  - Do NOT add water to the freezer meal bag, add that at time of pressure cooking
- Remove as much air as possible and seal. Add label to baggie and freeze.

Cooking Directions

1. Open, drain and rinse the black beans.
2. Place the chicken breasts in the electric pressure cooker insert with the hot water. Pour the black beans, salsa, and taco seasoning over the top.
3. Steam valve: Sealing.
4. Cook on: Manual/High for 15 minutes.
5. Release: Natural or Quick.
6. Once finished cooking, shred the chicken into the sauce. Season with salt and pepper to taste.
7. Prepare the salad with lettuce, shredded chicken and black beans and guacamole topping.
8. Prepare veggies.
9. Serve Instant Pot Chicken & Black Bean Taco Salad with guacamole and veggies.

Freeze, Thaw & Pressure Cook Instructions

Put baggie in the freezer and freeze up to 6 months in fridge freezer or 12 months in a deep freezer. Thaw in the fridge overnight, or a bowl of warm water for about 20 minutes, before adding contents of bag plus 1/2 cup hot water to electric pressure cooker insert. Pressure cook as directed.

If cooking freezer meal from partially thawed, add the hot water to the insert, add the frozen ingredients and adjust Pressure Cook time to 23 to 25 minutes.

Instant Pot Chicken Tikka Masala

Yield:	4 servings
Prep Time:	10 minutes
Cook Time:	15 minutes plus pressure build and release time

Ingredients

- 8 boneless chicken thighs
- 1/2 cup hot water
- 1 small white onion
- 1 small fresh ginger
- 28 oz. can crushed tomatoes
- 1 cup plain yogurt
- 3 tsp minced garlic
- 2 tsp garam masala
- Salt and pepper
- Garnish: chopped cilantro
- Side: rice
- Side: salad
- 1 gallon-size freezer baggie

Prepare to Freeze Instructions

- Cut chicken thighs into 1-inch pieces.
- Dice onions. Peel and slice the ginger (about 8 thin slices).
- In a large mixing bowl, whisk together crushed tomatoes, plain yogurt, minced garlic, garam masala and a few pinches of salt and pepper.
- Open can of crushed tomatoes.
- To gallon-size plastic freezer baggie in a round bowl/dish, add the following ingredients:
  - ○ Chicken pieces
  - ○ Onion and fresh ginger
  - ○ Prepared sauce
  - ○ Do NOT add water to the freezer meal bag, add that at time of pressure cooking
- Remove as much air as possible and seal. Add label to baggie and freeze.

Cooking Directions

1. Dice the onion. Peel and slice the ginger (about 8 thin slices).
2. Cut the chicken into 1-inch pieces and place into the electric pressure cooker insert with the hot water. Add the onion and ginger around the chicken.
3. In a large mixing bowl, whisk together the crushed tomatoes, yogurt, minced garlic, garam masala and a few pinches of salt and pepper. Pour over the chicken in the electric pressure cooker insert.
4. Steam valve: Sealing.
5. Cook on: Manual/High for 15 minutes.
6. Cook rice, as directed.
7. Prepare salad.
8. Serve Instant Pot Chicken Tikka Masala with cilantro garnish over rice with side salad.

Freeze, Thaw & Pressure Cook Instructions

Put baggie in the freezer and freeze up to 6 months in fridge freezer or 12 months in a deep freezer. Thaw in the fridge overnight, or a bowl of warm water for about 20 minutes, before adding contents of bag plus 1/2 cup hot water to electric pressure cooker insert. Pressure cook as directed.

If cooking freezer meal from partially thawed, add the hot water to the insert, add the frozen ingredients and adjust Pressure Cook time to 23 to 25 minutes.

Instant Pot Chickpea Beef Chili

Yield:	4 servings
Prep Time:	15 minutes
Cook Time:	15 minutes plus pressure build and release time

Ingredients

- 1 lb. ground beef
- 1 Tbsp minced onion
- 1 tsp garlic powder
- 15 oz. can chickpeas
- 15 oz. can diced tomatoes
- 2 cups beef broth
- 2 Tbsp chili powder
- Salt and pepper
- 1 cup hot water
- Garnish: shredded cheese
- Garnish: sour cream
- Side: veggies
- 1 gallon-size freezer baggie

Prepare to Freeze Instructions

- Brown ground beef, minced onion and garlic powder. Drain and let cool.
- Open can of diced tomatoes.
- Open and drain can of chickpeas.
- To gallon-size plastic freezer baggie in a round bowl/dish, add the following ingredients:
  - Cooled browned ground beef
  - Diced tomatoes
  - Drained chickpeas
  - 2 Tbsp chili powder
  - Salt and pepper
  - Do NOT add broth to the freezer meal bag, add that at time of pressure cooking
- Remove as much air as possible and seal. Add label to baggie and freeze.

Cooking Directions

1. Open and drain the chickpeas. Open the diced tomatoes.
2. In a large saucepan, brown the ground beef with the minced onion and garlic powder. Drain and add the browned ground beef to the pressure cooker insert.
3. Note: You can skip the skillet and brown the ground beef using the Saute Mode of your Instant Pot. Tap on Saute, adjust to More/High, and brown the ground beef with the minced onion and garlic powder. Drain, if needed, and return the browned ground beef to the insert.
4. Stir in the drained chickpeas, diced tomatoes, beef broth and chili powder into the electric pressure cooker insert. Season with salt and pepper to taste. Stir in the hot water.
5. Steam valve: Sealing.
6. Cook on: Manual/High for 15 minutes
7. Release: Natural or Quick.
8. Prepare veggies.
9. Serve Instant Pot Chickpea Beef Chili with sour cream and shredded cheese garnish, and veggies.

Freeze, Thaw & Pressure Cook Instructions

Put baggie in the freezer and freeze up to 6 months in fridge freezer or 12 months in a deep freezer. Thaw in the fridge overnight, or a bowl of warm water for about 20 minutes, before transferring to pressure cooker insert with 2 cups beef broth.

If cooking freezer meal from partially thawed, add the beef broth to the insert, add the frozen ingredients and adjust Pressure Cook time to 30 to 35 minutes.

Instant Pot Cilantro Lime Chicken

Yield: 4 servings
Prep Time: 10 minutes
Cook Time: 15 minutes plus pressure build and release time

Ingredients

- 2 lbs. boneless chicken thighs
- 1/2 cup hot water
- 1 Tbsp canola oil
- 2 limes
- 1 Tbsp brown sugar
- 4 tsp minced garlic
- 1 Tbsp chili powder
- 1/3 cup chopped cilantro
- Salt and pepper
- Side: rice
- Side: veggies
- 1 gallon-size freezer baggie

Prepare to Freeze Instructions

- Juice limes.
- Chop cilantro.
- In a large mixing bowl, whisk together canola oil, juice from limes, brown sugar, minced garlic, chili powder, chopped cilantro and salt and pepper.
- Into gallon-size plastic freezer baggie in a round bowl/dish, add the following ingredients:
  - Boneless chicken thighs
  - Prepared marinade
  - Do NOT add water to the freezer meal bag, add that at time of pressure cooking
- Remove as much air as possible and seal. Add label to baggie and freeze.

Cooking Directions

1. Juice both limes. Chop cilantro.
2. In a large mixing bowl, whisk together the canola oil, juice from 2 limes, brown sugar, minced garlic, chili powder and cilantro. Add a little salt and pepper and then whisk the marinade. Add the chicken thighs and coat them in the marinade. Put in the fridge and marinate for at least 30 minutes.
3. Cook rice, as directed.
4. Turn on the Instant Pot and set to Saute. Let warm up and then add the chicken thighs and marinade and saute for 4 minutes.
5. Then, if needed, add water or chicken stock so that the total liquid is at least 1 cup. Put the lid on and follow the cooking steps below.
6. Steam valve: Sealing.
7. Cook on: Manual/High for 15 minutes.
8. Release: Natural or Quick.
9. Prepare veggies and rice.
10. Serve Instant Pot Cilantro Lime Chicken with rice and veggies.

Freeze, Thaw & Pressure Cook Instructions

Put baggie in the freezer and freeze up to 6 months in fridge freezer or 12 months in a deep freezer. Thaw in the fridge overnight, or a bowl of warm water for about 20 minutes, before adding contents to electric pressure cooker insert. Saute and pressure cook as directed.

If cooking freezer meal from partially thawed, add the hot water to the insert, add the frozen ingredients and adjust Pressure Cook time to 23 to 25 minutes.

Instant Pot One-Pot Spaghetti

Yield: 4 servings
Prep Time: 15 minutes
Cook Time: 6 minutes plus pressure build and release time

Ingredients

- 1 lb. ground beef
- 1 Tbsp. minced onion
- 1 tsp. garlic powder
- 26 oz. jar marinara sauce
- 16 oz. spaghetti pasta
- 2 1/2 cups beef stock, chicken stock or water
- Parmesan cheese, as garnish
- Side salad
- 1 gallon-size freezer baggie

Prepare to Freeze Instructions

- Brown ground beef with minced onion and garlic powder. Let cool.
- To gallon-size plastic freezer baggie in a round bowl/dish, add the following ingredients:
  - Ground beef, browned and cooled
  - Jar spaghetti sauce
  - Salt and pepper
  - Do NOT add beef stock, chicken stock or water to the freezer meal bag, add that at time of pressure cooking
- Remove as much air as possible and seal. Add label to baggie and freeze.

Cooking Directions

1. Add the ground beef, minced onion, and garlic powder to the Instant Pot insert. Set on Saute mode and brown the ground beef in the insert. Once browned, stir in the marinara sauce.
2. Break the noodles in half or thirds and mix into the sauce and then pour the beef/chicken stock/water over the top. Give it a gentle stir and then press all the noodles into the liquid.
3. Close the lid, set to sealing.
4. Set on Manual, High Pressure and cook for 6 minutes.
5. Let naturally release for 5 minutes, then finish the release by setting to Venting.
6. The sauce will look too thin, but give it a stir and it will thicken up with the pasta and meat.
7. Serve Instant Pot One-Pot Spaghetti with Parmesan cheese garnish, and a side salad.

Freeze, Thaw & Pressure Cook Instructions

Put baggie in the freezer and freeze up to 6 months in fridge freezer or 12 months in a deep freezer. Thaw completely. Transfer to pressure cooker, then pressure cook as directed with pasta and 2 1/2 cups beef stock, chicken stock or water.

Instant Pot Cuban Chili

Yield:	4 servings
Prep Time:	15 minutes
Cook Time:	15 minutes plus pressure build and release time

Ingredients

- 1 lb. ground beef
- 1 Tbsp minced onion
- 1 tsp garlic powder
- 1 green bell pepper
- 15 oz. can diced tomatoes
- 1 Tbsp chili powder
- 1 tsp ground cumin
- 1 tsp dried oregano
- 1/2 tsp cinnamon
- 2 cups beef broth
- 1 cup raisins
- Salt and pepper
- 1 cup hot water
- Side: salad
- 1 gallon-size freezer baggie

Prepare to Freeze Instructions

- Brown ground beef with minced onion and garlic powder. Let cool.
- Seed and chop green bell peppers.
- Open and drain cans of diced tomatoes.
- To gallon-size plastic freezer baggie in a round bowl/dish, add the following ingredients:
  - Browned ground beef
  - Diced tomatoes
  - Chopped bell peppers
  - 1 Tbsp chili powder
  - 1 tsp ground cumin
  - 1 tsp dried oregano
  - 1/2 tsp cinnamon
  - Raisins
  - Do NOT add broth to the freezer meal bag, add that at time of pressure cooking
- Remove as much air as possible and seal. Add label to baggie and freeze.

Cooking Directions

1. Open and drain the can of diced tomatoes.
2. Seed and chop the green bell pepper.
3. In a large saucepan, brown the ground beef with the minced onion and garlic powder. Drain and add the browned ground beef to the pressure cooker insert.
4. Note: You can skip the skillet and brown the ground beef using the Saute Mode of your Instant Pot. Tap on Saute, adjust to More/High, and brown the ground beef with the minced onion and garlic powder. Drain, if needed, and return the browned ground beef to the insert.
5. Stir in the chopped bell pepper, diced tomatoes, chili powder, ground cumin, dried oregano, cinnamon and hot water into the electric pressure cooker insert.
6. Stir in the beef broth and raisins. Season with salt and pepper to taste.
7. Steam valve: Sealing.
8. Cook on: Manual/High for 15 minutes.
9. Release: Natural or Quick.
10. Prepare the salad.
11. Serve Instant Pot Cuban Chili with salad.

Freeze, Thaw & Pressure Cook Instructions

Put baggie in the freezer and freeze up to 6 months in fridge freezer or 12 months in a deep freezer. Thaw in the fridge overnight, or a bowl of warm water for about 20 minutes, before transferring to pressure cooker insert with 2 cups beef broth. Pressure cook as directed.

If cooking freezer meal from partially thawed, add the beef broth to the insert, add the frozen ingredients and adjust Pressure Cook time to 30 to 35 minutes.

Instant Pot Dr. Pepper Pulled Pork

Yield:	4 servings
Prep Time:	10 minutes
Cook Time:	40 minutes plus pressure build and release time

Ingredients

- 2 lbs pork roast
- 1/2 cup hot water
- 1/2 small red onion
- Salt and pepper
- 12 oz. can Dr. Pepper
- 16 oz. BBQ sauce
- 8 hamburger buns
- Side: Coleslaw salad kit
- Side: chips
- 1 gallon-size freezer baggie

Prepare to Freeze Instructions

- Thinly slice red onion.
- To gallon-size plastic freezer baggie in a round bowl/dish, add the following ingredients:
  - Pork roast
  - Red onion slices
  - Salt and pepper
  - 12 oz. can Dr. Pepper
  - 16 oz. BBQ sauce
  - Do NOT add water to the freezer meal bag, add that at time of pressure cooking
- Remove as much air as possible and seal. Add label to baggie and freeze.

Cooking Directions

1. Thinly slice the red onion.
2. Place the pork roast and red onion slices into the electric pressure cooker insert with the hot water. Sprinkle with salt and pepper. Pour the Dr. Pepper and BBQ sauce over the pork roast.
3. Steam valve: Sealing.
4. Cook on: Manual/High for 40 minutes.
5. Release: Natural or Quick.
6. Prepare the coleslaw salad just before serving.
7. Once the pork roast is cooked, shred the meat with 2 forks and toss with the sauce. Spoon shredded pork onto hamburger buns and top with Coleslaw.
8. Serve Instant Pot Dr. Pepper Pulled Pork with chips.

Freeze, Thaw & Pressure Cook Instructions

Put baggie in the freezer and freeze up to 6 months in fridge freezer or 12 months in a deep freezer. Thaw in the fridge overnight, or a bowl of warm water for about 20 minutes, before adding contents of bag plus 1/2 cup hot water to electric pressure cooker insert. Pressure cook as directed.

If cooking freezer meal from partially thawed, add the hot water to the insert, add the frozen ingredients and adjust Pressure Cook time to 65 minutes.

Instant Pot Garlic Lime Chicken

Yield:	4 servings
Prep Time:	10 minutes
Cook Time:	15 minutes plus pressure build and release time

Ingredients

- 4 small boneless chicken breasts
- 1/2 cup hot water
- 1/4 cup lime juice
- 1/4 cup olive oil
- 1 Tbsp minced garlic
- Salt and pepper
- Side: rice
- Side: salad
- 1 gallon-size freezer baggie

Prepare to Freeze Instructions

- To gallon-size plastic freezer baggie in a round bowl/dish, add the following ingredients:
  - Chicken breasts
  - 1/4 cup lime juice
  - 1/4 cup olive oil
  - 1 Tbsp minced garlic
  - Salt and pepper
  - Do NOT add water to the freezer meal bag, add that at time of pressure cooking
- Remove as much air as possible and seal. Add label to baggie and freeze.

Cooking Directions

1. In a mixing bowl, whisk together the lime juice, olive oil, minced garlic, salt and pepper. Add the chicken breasts and coat with the marinade. Place in the fridge and let marinate for at least 2 hours.
2. Place the chicken and marinade into the electric pressure cooker insert with the hot water.
3. Steam valve: Sealing.
4. Cook on: Manual/High for 15 minutes.
5. Release: Natural or Quick.
6. Cook the rice, as directed.
7. Prepare the salad.
8. Serve Instant Pot Garlic Lime Chicken over rice with salad.

Freeze, Thaw & Pressure Cook Instructions

Put baggie in the freezer and freeze up to 6 months in fridge freezer or 12 months in a deep freezer. Thaw in the fridge overnight, or a bowl of warm water for about 20 minutes. Transfer the chicken and marinade to electric pressure cooker insert and pressure cook as directed.

If cooking freezer meal from partially thawed, add the 1/2 cup hot water to the insert, add the frozen ingredients and adjust Pressure Cook time to 23 to 25 minutes.

Instant Pot Green Chile Chicken Street Tacos

Yield:	4 servings
Prep Time:	10 minutes
Cook Time:	15 minutes plus pressure build and release time

Ingredients

- 2 large boneless chicken breasts
- 4 boneless chicken thighs
- 1/2 cup hot water
- 1 cup green salsa
- 4 oz. can diced green chiles
- 1 Tbsp ground cumin
- Salt and pepper
- 12 corn tortillas
- Garnish: sour cream
- Garnish: chopped cilantro
- Side: veggies
- 1 gallon-size freezer baggie

Prepare to Freeze Instructions

- Open 2 cans of green chilies.
- To gallon-size plastic freezer baggie in a round bowl/dish, add the following ingredients:
  - 2 large boneless chicken breasts
  - 4 boneless chicken thighs
  - 1 cup green salsa
  - 4 oz. can green chiles
  - 1 Tbsp ground cumin
  - Salt and pepper
  - Do NOT add water to the freezer meal bag, add that at time of pressure cooking
- Remove as much air as possible and seal. Add label to baggie and freeze.

Cooking Directions

1. Open the green chiles.
2. Place the chicken breasts and chicken thighs into the electric pressure cooker insert with the hot water. Add the green salsa, green chilies, ground cumin, salt and pepper on top of the chicken.
3. Steam valve: Sealing.
4. Cook on: Manual/High for 15 minutes.
5. Release: Natural or Quick.
6. Once finished cooking, shred the chicken with 2 forks and mix into the green chile sauce.
7. Spoon the shredded chicken into corn tortillas.
8. Prepare veggies.
9. Serve Instant Pot Green Chile Chicken Street Tacos with sour cream and cilantro garnish with veggies.

Freeze, Thaw & Pressure Cook Instructions

Put baggie in the freezer and freeze up to 6 months in fridge freezer or 12 months in a deep freezer. Thaw in the fridge overnight, or a bowl of warm water for about 20 minutes, before adding contents of bag plus 1/2 cup hot water to electric pressure cooker insert. Pressure cook as directed.

If cooking freezer meal from partially thawed, add the hot water to the insert, add the frozen ingredients and adjust Pressure Cook time to 23 to 25 minutes.

Instant Pot Green Pepper Chili

Yield:	4 servings
Prep Time:	5 minutes
Cook Time:	15 minutes plus pressure build and release time

Ingredients

- 1 lb. ground beef
- 1 Tbsp minced onion
- 1 tsp garlic powder
- 2 green bell peppers
- 15 oz. can diced tomatoes
- 6 oz. can tomato paste
- 15 oz. can black beans
- 15 oz. can red kidney beans
- 2 tsp minced garlic
- 1 Tbsp chili powder
- Salt and pepper
- 1 cup hot water
- Side: corn tortilla chips
- Side: fruit
- 1 gallon-size freezer baggie

Prepare to Freeze Instructions

- Brown ground beef with minced onion and garlic powder.
- Seed and chop green bell peppers.
- Open cans of diced tomatoes and tomato paste.
- Open, drain and rinse cans of black beans and red kidney beans.
- To gallon-size plastic freezer baggie in a round bowl/dish, add the following ingredients:
  - Browned ground beef
  - Green bell peppers
  - Diced tomatoes
  - Tomato paste
  - Black beans, drained
  - Red kidney beans, drained
  - 2 tsp minced garlic
  - 1 Tbsp chili powder
  - Salt and pepper
  - Do NOT add water to the freezer meal bag, add that at time of pressure cooking
- Remove as much air as possible and seal. Add label to baggie and freeze.

Cooking Directions

1. In a large skillet, brown the ground beef with the minced onion and garlic powder. Drain and add to pressure cooker insert.
2. Note: You can skip the skillet and brown the ground beef using the Saute Mode of your Instant Pot. Tap on Saute, adjust to More/High, and brown the ground beef with the minced onion and garlic powder. Drain, if needed, and return the browned ground beef to the insert.
3. Seed and chop the green bell peppers.
4. Open, drain, and rinse the black beans and red kidney beans.
5. Add the chopped bell peppers, diced tomatoes, tomato paste, black beans, red kidney beans and minced garlic to the ground beef mixture.
6. Stir together and stir in the chili powder, salt and pepper and hot water.
7. Steam valve: Sealing.
8. Pressure Cook: Manual/High for 15 minutes.
9. Release: Natural or Quick.
10. Prepare the fruit.
11. Serve Instant Pot Green Pepper Chili with fruit and chips.

Freeze, Thaw & Pressure Cook Instructions

Put baggie in the freezer and freeze up to 6 months in fridge freezer or 12 months in a deep freezer. Thaw in the fridge overnight, or a bowl of warm water for about 20 minutes, before transferring to pressure cooker insert with 1 cup hot water and pressure cook as directed.

If cooking freezer meal from partially thawed, add the hot water to the insert, add the frozen ingredients and adjust Pressure Cook time to 30 to 35 minutes.

Instant Pot Herbed Pork Tenderloin

Yield:	4 servings
Prep Time:	10 minutes
Cook Time:	40 minutes plus pressure build and release time

Ingredients

- 2 lbs. pork tenderloin
- 1 cup hot water
- Salt and pepper
- 1 Tbsp minced onion
- 1 tsp minced garlic
- 1 tsp dried oregano
- 1 tsp dried basil
- 1 tsp dried rosemary
- Side: veggies
- Side: dinner rolls
- 1 gallon-size freezer baggie

Prepare to Freeze Instructions

- In a small bowl, toss together minced onion, minced garlic, oregano, basil, and rosemary.
- To gallon-size plastic freezer baggie in a round bowl/dish, add the following ingredients:
  - Pork tenderloin
  - Salt and pepper
  - Herb mixture
  - Do NOT add water to the freezer meal bag, add that at time of pressure cooking
- Remove as much air as possible and seal. Add label to baggie and freeze.

Cooking Directions

1. Place the pork tenderloin into the electric pressure cooker insert with the hot water. Season with salt and pepper.
2. In a small bowl, toss together the minced onion, minced garlic, dried oregano, dried basil and dried rosemary. Add the herb mixture directly onto the pork roast, pressing lightly.
3. Steam valve: Sealing.
4. Cook on: Manual/High for 40 minutes.
5. Release: Natural or Quick.
6. Once finished cooking, slice the pork roast. Season with salt and pepper to taste.
7. Prepare veggies.
8. Warm the dinner rolls.
9. Serve Instant Pot Herb Pork Tenderloin with veggies and dinner rolls.

Freeze, Thaw & Pressure Cook Instructions

Put baggie in the freezer and freeze up to 6 months in fridge freezer or 12 months in a deep freezer. Thaw in the fridge overnight, or a bowl of warm water for about 20 minutes, before adding contents of bag plus 1 cup hot water to electric pressure cooker insert. Pressure cook as directed.

If cooking freezer meal from partially thawed, add the hot water to the insert, add the frozen ingredients and adjust Pressure Cook time to 65 minutes.

Instant Pot Herbed Turkey Breast

Yield: 4 servings
Prep Time: 5 minutes
Cook Time: 10 minutes plus pressure build and release time

Ingredients

- 1 cup chicken stock
- 3 lbs. boneless turkey breast
- Salt and pepper
- 2 Tbsp herb seasoning blend
- 1 gallon-size freezer baggie

Prepare to Freeze Instructions

- To gallon-size plastic freezer baggie in a round bowl/dish, add the following ingredients:
  - Boneless turkey breast
  - Salt and pepper
  - 2 Tbsp herb seasoning blend
  - Do NOT add chicken stock to the freezer meal bag, add that at time of pressure cooking
- Remove as much air from bag as possible, add label and freeze.

Cooking Directions

1. Add the chicken stock to the Instant Pot insert. Place the rack that came with the appliance or a steam rack into the insert.
2. Season the turkey breast with salt and pepper on both sides. Place onto the steam rack in the insert. Sprinkle the herb seasoning blend directly onto the turkey breast, covering and coating it well.
3. Steam valve: Sealing.
4. Cook on: Manual/High for 8-10 minutes. For thinner breast fillets, cook for 8 minutes and for thicker fillets, cook for 10 minutes.
5. Release: Natural or Quick.
6. Remove the turkey breast to slice and serve.
7. Optional: Ladle out the juices from the base and skim off the fat and then whisk in some flour or cornstarch to make a gravy.
8. Serve Instant Pot Herbed Turkey Breast with favorite side dishes.

Freeze, Thaw & Pressure Cook Instructions

Put baggie in the freezer and freeze up to 6 months in fridge freezer or 12 months in a deep freezer. Thaw in the fridge overnight, or a bowl of warm water for about 20 minutes, before transferring to pressure cooker insert with 1 cup chicken stock. Pressure cook as directed.

If cooking freezer meal from partially thawed, add the chicken stock to the insert, add the frozen ingredients and adjust Pressure Cook time to 23 to 25 minutes.

Instant Pot Honey Garlic Chicken

Yield:	4 servings
Prep Time:	10 minutes
Cook Time:	15 minutes plus pressure build and release time

Ingredients

- 4 small boneless chicken breasts
- 1/2 cup hot water
- 1/2 cup soy sauce
- 1/2 cup honey
- 1/4 cup teriyaki sauce
- 2 Tbsp rice vinegar
- 1 tsp sesame oil
- 2 tsp minced garlic
- 1 tsp minced onion
- 1 tsp ground ginger
- 2 Tbsp cornstarch
- Garnish: sliced green onions
- Side: rice
- Side: salad
- 1 gallon-size freezer baggie

Prepare to Freeze Instructions

- In a small mixing bowl, whisk together soy sauce, honey, teriyaki sauce, rice vinegar, sesame oil, minced garlic, minced onion, and ground ginger.
- To gallon-size plastic freezer baggie in a round bowl/dish, add the following ingredients:
  - Chicken breasts
  - Salt and pepper
  - Prepared marinade
  - Do NOT add the cornstarch or water to freezer bag
- Remove as much air as possible and seal. Add label to baggie and freeze.

Cooking Directions

1. Place the chicken into the electric pressure cooker insert with the hot water. Season with salt and pepper.
2. In a small mixing bowl, whisk together the soy sauce, honey, teriyaki sauce, rice vinegar, sesame oil, minced garlic, minced onion, and ground ginger. Do NOT add the cornstarch.
3. Steam valve: Sealing.
4. Cook on: Manual/High for 15 minutes.
5. Release: Natural or Quick.
6. After cooking, shred the chicken with 2 forks. Then mix the cornstarch with the same amount of water and swirl into the sauce.
7. Cook the rice, as directed.
8. Prepare the salad.
9. Serve Instant Pot Honey Garlic Chicken over rice with side salad.

Freeze, Thaw & Pressure Cook Instructions

Put baggie in the freezer and freeze up to 6 months in fridge freezer or 12 months in a deep freezer. Thaw in the fridge overnight, or a bowl of warm water for about 20 minutes, before adding the contents of bag plus 1/2 cup hot water to electric pressure cooker insert. Pressure cook as directed and swirl in the cornstarch at the end of pressure cooking as noted.

If cooking freezer meal from partially thawed, add the hot water to the insert, add the frozen ingredients and adjust Pressure Cook time to 23 to 25 minutes.

Instant Pot Island Chicken

Yield:	4 servings
Prep Time:	10 minutes
Cook Time:	15 minutes plus pressure build and release time

Ingredients

- 4 small boneless chicken breasts
- Salt and pepper
- 1 cup orange juice
- 1/2 cup lime juice
- 1/4 cup brown sugar
- 1 Tbsp ground cumin
- 1 tsp paprika
- 20 oz. can pineapple slices
- Side: rice
- Side: veggies
- 1 gallon-size freezer baggie

Prepare to Freeze Instructions

- To gallon-size plastic freezer baggie in a round bowl/dish, add the following ingredients:
  - Chicken breasts
  - Salt and pepper
  - 1 cup orange juice
  - 1/2 cup lime juice
  - 1/4 cup brown sugar
  - 1 Tbsp cumin
  - 1 tsp paprika
  - Sliced pineapple
  - Do NOT add water to the freezer meal bag, add that at time of pressure cooking
- Remove as much air as possible and seal. Add label to baggie and freeze.

Cooking Directions

1. Place the chicken breasts into the base of Instant Pot or electric pressure cooker and season with salt and pepper.
2. In a large mixing bowl, whisk together the orange juice, lime juice, brown sugar, ground cumin, and paprika.
3. Pour the marinade over the chicken, then add the pineapple slices around and on top of the chicken and marinade. If needed, add chicken stock or water so total liquid is at least 1 cup.
4. Steam valve: Sealing.
5. Cook on: Manual/High for 15 minutes.
6. Release: Natural or Quick.
7. Cook the rice as directed.
8. Prepare the veggies.
9. Serve Instant Pot Island Chicken over rice with veggies.

Freeze, Thaw & Pressure Cook Instructions

Put baggie in the freezer and freeze up to 6 months in fridge freezer or 12 months in a deep freezer. Thaw in the fridge overnight, or a bowl of warm water for about 20 minutes, before transferring to pressure cooker insert with hot water. Pressure cook as directed.

If cooking freezer meal from partially thawed, add the hot water to the insert, add the frozen ingredients and adjust Pressure Cook time to 23 to 25 minutes.

Instant Pot Italian Chicken & Potatoes

Yield:	4 servings
Prep Time:	5 minutes
Cook Time:	15 minutes plus pressure build and release time

Ingredients

- 4 small boneless chicken breasts
- 1/2 cup hot water
- 2 lbs. baby potatoes
- 1 lb. baby carrots
- 15 oz. can diced tomatoes
- 2 Tbsp Italian seasoning
- Salt and pepper
- Side: salad
- 1 gallon-size freezer baggie

Prepare to Freeze Instructions

- To gallon-size plastic freezer baggie in a round bowl/dish, add the following ingredients:
  - Chicken breasts
  - Baby potatoes
  - Baby carrots
  - Canned diced tomatoes, undrained
  - 2 Tbsp Italian seasoning
  - Salt and pepper
  - Do NOT add water to the freezer meal bag, add that at time of pressure cooking
- Remove as much air as possible and seal. Add label to baggie and freeze.

Cooking Directions

1. Place the chicken into the electric pressure cooker insert with the hot water. Add the baby potatoes and baby carrots around and on top of the chicken. Pour the diced tomatoes and their juices over top of the chicken-potatoes-carrots. Sprinkle the Italian seasoning over top. Sprinkle a little salt and pepper over the top.
2. Steam valve: Sealing.
3. Cook on: Manual/High for 15 minutes
4. Release: Natural or Quick.
5. Prepare salad.
6. Serve Instant Pot Italian Chicken & Potatoes with side salad.

Freeze, Thaw & Pressure Cook Instructions

Put baggie in the freezer and freeze up to 6 months in fridge freezer or 12 months in a deep freezer. Thaw in the fridge overnight, or a bowl of warm water for about 20 minutes, before adding contents of bag plus 1/2 cup hot water to electric pressure cooker insert. Pressure cook as directed.

If cooking freezer meal from partially thawed, add the hot water to the insert, add the frozen ingredients and adjust Pressure Cook time to 23 to 25 minutes.

Instant Pot Jamaican Pork Chops

Yield:	4 servings
Prep Time:	5 minutes
Cook Time:	20 minutes plus pressure build and release time

Ingredients

- 4 boneless pork chops
- 1/2 cup hot water
- Salt and pepper
- 1 Tbsp canola oil
- 8 oz. can crushed pineapple
- 1 Tbsp Jerk seasoning
- 1 Tbsp brown sugar
- Side: rice
- Side: salad
- 1 gallon-size freezer baggie

Prepare to Freeze Instructions

- Open and drain can of crushed pineapple.
- To gallon-size plastic freezer baggie in a round bowl/dish, add the following ingredients:
  - Pork chops
  - Salt and pepper
  - Crushed pineapple
  - 1 Tbsp Jerk seasoning
  - 1 Tbsp brown sugar
  - Do NOT add water to the freezer meal bag, add that at time of pressure cooking
- Remove as much air as possible and seal. Add label to baggie and freeze.

Cooking Directions

1. Cook the rice, as directed.
2. Open and drain the canned crushed pineapple.
3. Season both sides of the pork chops with salt and pepper.
4. Add the pork chops into the electric pressure cooker insert with the hot water.
5. Mix together the crushed pineapple, Jerk seasoning and brown sugar. Spread on top of and around the pork chops in the electric pressure cooker insert.
6. Steam valve: Sealing.
7. Cook on: Manual/High for 20 minutes.
8. Release: Natural or Quick.
9. Prepare the salad.
10. Serve Instant Pot Jamaican Pork Chops with rice and salad.

Freeze, Thaw & Pressure Cook Instructions

Put baggie in the freezer and freeze up to 6 months in fridge freezer or 12 months in a deep freezer. Thaw in the fridge overnight, or a bowl of warm water for about 20 minutes, before adding contents of bag plus 1/2 cup hot water to electric pressure cooker insert. Pressure cook as directed.

If cooking freezer meal from partially thawed, add the hot water to the insert, add the frozen ingredients and adjust Pressure Cook time to 24 minutes.

Instant Pot Jerk Pulled Pork Sliders

Yield: 4 servings
Prep Time: 5 minutes
Cook Time: 40 minutes plus pressure build and release time

Ingredients

- 2 lbs pork roast
- 1/2 cup hot water
- Salt and pepper
- 1/4 cup lime juice
- 3 Tbsp Jerk seasoning
- 1 tsp garlic powder
- 1 tsp onion powder
- 1 tsp ground cumin
- 1 tsp brown sugar
- 1 8 oz. can sliced pineapple
- 12 slider buns
- Garnish: sliced green onions
- Side: fruit
- Side: chips
- 1 gallon-size freezer baggie

Prepare to Freeze Instructions

- Open and drain 2 cans of sliced pineapple.
- To gallon-size plastic freezer baggie in a round bowl/dish, add the following ingredients:
  - Pork roast
  - Salt and pepper
  - 1/4 cup lime juice
  - 3 Tbsp Jerk seasoning
  - 1 tsp garlic powder
  - 1 tsp onion powder
  - 1 tsp ground cumin
  - 1 tsp brown sugar
  - Canned sliced pineapple
  - Do NOT add water to the freezer meal bag, add that at time of pressure cooking
- Remove as much air as possible and seal. Add label to baggie and freeze.

Cooking Directions

1. Place the pork roast into the electric pressure cooker insert with the hot water and season with salt and pepper. Pour the lime juice on and around the pork. Season with the Jerk seasoning, garlic powder, onion powder, ground cumin and brown sugar. Place the pineapple slices over the top.
2. Steam valve: Sealing.
3. Cook on: Manual/High for 40 minutes.
4. Release: Natural or Quick.
5. Once finished cooking, shred the pork with 2 forks and mix into the sauce. Strain before adding the pork to the sliders.
6. Assemble sliders by adding the shredded pork and sliced green onion garnish.
7. Prepare fruit.
8. Serve Instant Pot Jerk Pulled Pork Sliders with fruit and chips.

Freeze, Thaw & Pressure Cook Instructions

Put baggie in the freezer and freeze up to 6 months in fridge freezer or 12 months in a deep freezer. Thaw in the fridge overnight, or a bowl of warm water for about 20 minutes, before adding contents of bag plus 1/2 cup hot water to electric pressure cooker insert. Pressure cook as directed.

If cooking freezer meal from partially thawed, add the hot water to the insert, add the frozen ingredients and adjust Pressure Cook time to 65 minutes.

Instant Pot Mango Salsa Chicken

Yield: 4 servings
Prep Time: 10 minutes
Cook Time: 15 minutes plus pressure build and release time

Ingredients

- 2 large boneless chicken breasts
- 1/2 cup hot water
- 3 ripe mangos
- 1 cup salsa
- Salt and pepper
- Garnish: chopped cilantro
- Side: rice
- Side: veggies
- 1 gallon-size freezer baggie

Prepare to Freeze Instructions

- Seed and slice mangoes.
- To gallon-size plastic freezer baggie in a round bowl/dish, add the following ingredients:
  - Chicken breasts
  - Sliced mango
  - 1 cup salsa
  - Salt and pepper
  - Do NOT add water to the freezer meal bag, add that at time of pressure cooking
- Remove as much air as possible and seal. Add label to baggie and freeze.

Cooking Directions

1. Seed and slice the mango.
2. Add the chicken breasts into the electric pressure cooker insert with the hot water.
3. Add in the sliced mango, salsa, salt and pepper into the electric pressure cooker insert.
4. Steam valve: Sealing.
5. Cook on: Manual/High for 15 minutes.
6. Release: Natural or Quick.
7. Cook rice, as directed.
8. Prepare veggies.
9. Chop the cilantro garnish.
10. Serve Instant Pot Mango Salsa Chicken topped with cilantro garnish over rice with veggies.

Freeze, Thaw & Pressure Cook Instructions

Put baggie in the freezer and freeze up to 6 months in fridge freezer or 12 months in a deep freezer. Thaw in the fridge overnight, or a bowl of warm water for about 20 minutes, before adding contents of bag plus 1/2 cup hot water to electric pressure cooker insert. Pressure cook as directed.

If cooking freezer meal from partially thawed, add the hot water to the insert, add the frozen ingredients and adjust Pressure Cook time to 23 to 25 minutes.

Instant Pot New Brunswick Stew

Yield:	4 servings
Prep Time:	15 minutes
Cook Time:	30 minutes plus pressure build and release time

Ingredients

- 4 boneless chicken thighs
- 4 boneless pork chops
- 1/2 cup hot water
- 1 small white onion
- 1 tsp minced garlic
- 1 cup BBQ sauce
- 15 oz. can crushed tomatoes
- 15 oz. can corn
- 15 oz. can lima beans
- 2 cups chicken stock
- Salt and pepper
- Side: salad
- Side: dinner rolls
- 1 gallon-size freezer baggie

Prepare to Freeze Instructions

- Chop onion.
- Open can of crushed tomatoes. Open and drain cans of corn and lima or butter beans.
- To gallon-size plastic freezer baggie in a round bowl/dish, add the following ingredients:
  - Chicken thighs
  - Pork chops
  - Half of the chopped onion
  - 1 tsp minced garlic
  - 1 cup BBQ sauce
  - Crushed tomatoes
  - Corn
  - Lima or butter beans
  - Salt and pepper
  - Do NOT add water or chicken stock to the freezer meal bag, add that at time of pressure cooking
- Remove as much air as possible and seal. Add label to baggie and freeze.

Cooking Directions

1. Open the can of crushed tomatoes, corn and lima or butter beans. Drain the corn and beans.
2. Chop the onion.
3. Add the chicken thighs, pork chops, chopped onion, minced garlic, BBQ sauce, crushed tomatoes, corn, beans, chicken stock, and hot water into the electric pressure cooker insert. Add a little salt and pepper.
4. Steam valve: Sealing.
5. Cook on: Manual/High for 30 minutes.
6. Release: Natural or Quick.
7. Once finished cooking, use 2 forks and shred the chicken and pork chops into the stew.
8. Prepare the salad.
9. Warm the dinner rolls.
10. Serve Instant Pot New Brunswick Stew with salad and dinner rolls.

Freeze, Thaw & Pressure Cook Instructions

Put baggie in the freezer and freeze up to 6 months in fridge freezer or 12 months in a deep freezer. Thaw in the fridge overnight, or a bowl of warm water for about 20 minutes, before adding contents of bag plus 1/2 cup hot water and 2 cups chicken stock to electric pressure cooker insert. Pressure cook as directed.

If cooking freezer meal from partially thawed, add the hot water and chicken stock to the insert, add the frozen ingredients and adjust Pressure Cook time to 23 to 25 minutes.

Instant Pot Peach Orange Pork Chops

Yield:	4 servings
Prep Time:	5 minutes
Cook Time:	15 minutes plus pressure build and release time

Ingredients

- 4 boneless pork chops
- 1/2 cup hot water
- Salt and pepper
- 1/4 cup peach preserves
- 1/4 cup orange marmalade
- 2 Tbsp Dijon mustard
- 1 tsp soy sauce
- Side: dinner rolls
- Side: salad
- 1 gallon-size freezer baggie

Prepare to Freeze Instructions

- In a small mixing bowl, combine the peach preserves, orange marmalade, Dijon mustard and sauce.
- To gallon-size plastic freezer baggie in a round bowl/dish, add the following ingredients:
  - Pork chops
  - Peach-orange sauce
  - Do NOT add water to the freezer meal bag, add that at time of pressure cooking
- Remove as much air as possible and seal. Add label to baggie and freeze.

Cooking Directions

1. Place the pork chops into the electric pressure cooker insert with the hot water. Season with salt and pepper.
2. In a small mixing bowl, combine the 1/4 cup peach preserves, 1/4 cup orange marmalade, 2 Tbsp Dijon mustard and 1 tsp soy sauce. Place directly on top of the pork chops.
3. Steam valve: Sealing.
4. Cook on: Manual/High for 15 minutes.
5. Release: Natural or Quick.
6. Warm the dinner rolls.
7. Prepare the salad.
8. Serve Instant Pot Peach Orange Pork Chops with dinner rolls and salad.

Freeze, Thaw & Pressure Cook Instructions

Put baggie in the freezer and freeze up to 6 months in fridge freezer or 12 months in a deep freezer. Thaw in the fridge overnight, or a bowl of warm water for about 20 minutes, before adding contents of bag plus 1/2 cup hot water to electric pressure cooker insert. Pressure cook as directed.

If cooking freezer meal from partially thawed, add the hot water to the insert, add the frozen ingredients and adjust Pressure Cook time to 24 minutes.

Instant Pot Plum Pork Tenderloin

Yield:	4 servings
Prep Time:	10 minutes
Cook Time:	40 minutes plus pressure build and release time

Ingredients

- 2 lbs pork tenderloin
- 1/2 cup hot water
- Salt and pepper
- 9 oz. jar plum sauce
- 1 tsp cinnamon
- 1 tsp ground allspice
- 2 plums
- Side: salad
- Side: rice
- 1 gallon-size freezer baggie

Prepare to Freeze Instructions

- Seed and slice plums into small wedges.
- To gallon-size plastic freezer baggie in a round bowl/dish, add the following ingredients:
  - Pork tenderloin
  - Salt and pepper
  - 9 oz. jar plum sauce
  - 1 tsp cinnamon
  - 1 tsp ground allspice
  - plum wedges
  - Do NOT add water to the freezer meal bag, add that at time of pressure cooking
- Remove as much air as possible and seal. Add label to baggie and freeze.

Cooking Directions

1. Slice the plums into small wedges.
2. Place the pork tenderloin into the electric pressure cooker insert with the hot water. Season with salt and pepper. Pour the plum sauce over the top and then sprinkle the cinnamon and allspice over the plum sauce. Add the plum slices.
3. Steam valve: Sealing.
4. Cook on: Manual/High for 40 minutes.
5. Release: Natural or Quick.
6. Cook the rice, as directed.
7. Prepare the salad.
8. Serve Instant Pot Plum Pork Tenderloin over rice with side salad.

Freeze, Thaw & Pressure Cook Instructions

Put baggie in the freezer and freeze up to 6 months in fridge freezer or 12 months in a deep freezer. Thaw in the fridge overnight, or a bowl of warm water for about 20 minutes, before adding contents of bag plus 1/2 cup hot water to electric pressure cooker insert. Pressure cook as directed. Add an extra 5-10 minutes if you have an extra thick pork tenderloin.

If cooking freezer meal from partially thawed, add the hot water to the insert, add the frozen ingredients and adjust Pressure Cook time to 65 minutes.

Instant Pot Pork Carnitas Nachos

Yield:	4 servings
Prep Time:	5 minutes
Cook Time:	40 minutes plus pressure build and release time

Ingredients

- 2 lbs. pork roast
- 1/2 cup hot water
- Salt and pepper
- 1 packet taco seasoning
- 1/4 cup lime juice
- 1 bag corn tortilla chips
- 2 cups shredded mozzarella cheese
- Garnish: chopped cilantro
- Side: veggies
- 1 gallon-size freezer baggie

Prepare to Freeze Instructions

- To gallon-size plastic freezer baggie in a round bowl/dish, add the following ingredients:
  - Pork roast
  - Salt and pepper
  - 1 packet taco seasoning
  - 1/4 cup lime juice
  - Do NOT add water to the freezer meal bag, add that at time of pressure cooking
- Remove as much air as possible and seal. Add label to baggie and freeze.

Cooking Directions

1. Place the pork roast into the electric pressure cooker insert with the hot water. Season with salt and pepper. Sprinkle the taco seasoning and lime juice over the top.
2. Steam valve: Sealing.
3. Cook on: Manual/High for 40 minutes.
4. Release: Natural or Quick.
5. Shred the pork roast when it's finished cooking.
6. Assemble nachos with corn tortillas chips, shredded pork and shredded cheese. Top with chopped cilantro garnish. If needed, place in the microwave or oven to melt the cheese.
7. Prepare veggies.
8. Serve Instant Pot Pork Carnitas Nachos with side of veggies.

Freeze, Thaw & Pressure Cook Instructions

Put baggie in the freezer and freeze up to 6 months in fridge freezer or 12 months in a deep freezer. Thaw in the fridge overnight, or a bowl of warm water for about 20 minutes, before adding contents of bag plus 1/2 cup hot water to electric pressure cooker insert. Pressure cook as directed.

If cooking freezer meal from partially thawed, add the hot water to the insert, add the frozen ingredients and adjust Pressure Cook time to 65 minutes.

Instant Pot Pulled Pork Ragu

Yield:	4 servings
Prep Time:	10 minutes
Cook Time:	40 minutes plus pressure build and release time

Ingredients

- 2 lbs pork tenderloin
- 1/2 cup hot water
- Salt and pepper
- 28 oz. can crushed tomatoes
- 7 oz. jar red peppers
- 3 tsp minced garlic
- 2 Tbsp Italian seasoning
- Side: pasta
- Side: salad
- 1 gallon-size freezer baggie

Prepare to Freeze Instructions

- Open can of crushed tomatoes.
- Open and drain jar of roasted red peppers.
- To gallon-size plastic freezer baggie in a round bowl/dish, add the following ingredients:
  - Pork tenderloin
  - Salt and pepper
  - Crushed tomatoes
  - Roasted red peppers
  - 3 tsp minced garlic
  - 2 Tbsp Italian seasoning
  - Do NOT add water to the freezer meal bag, add that at time of pressure cooking
- Remove as much air as possible and seal. Add label to baggie and freeze.

Cooking Directions

1. Open the can of crushed tomatoes. Drain the jar of roasted red peppers.
2. Place the pork tenderloin into the base of the electric pressure cooker insert with the hot water and season with salt and pepper. Pour the crushed tomatoes, drained roasted red peppers, minced garlic and Italian seasoning over the pork tenderloin.
3. Steam valve: Sealing.
4. Cook on: Manual/High for 40 minutes.
5. Release: Natural or Quick.
6. Once finished cooking, shred the pork with 2 forks and mix into the ragu sauce.
7. Cook the pasta as directed.
8. Prepare the salad.
9. Serve Instant Pot Pulled Pork Ragu over pasta with salad.

Freeze, Thaw & Pressure Cook Instructions

Put baggie in the freezer and freeze up to 6 months in fridge freezer or 12 months in a deep freezer. Thaw in the fridge overnight, or a bowl of warm water for about 20 minutes, before adding contents of bag plus 1/2 cup hot water to electric pressure cooker insert. Pressure cook as directed.

If cooking freezer meal from partially thawed, add the hot water to the insert, add the frozen ingredients and adjust Pressure Cook time to 65 minutes.

Instant Pot Pumpkin Chili

Yield:	4 servings
Prep Time:	15 minutes
Cook Time:	15 minutes plus pressure build and release time

Ingredients

- 1 lb. ground beef
- 1 Tbsp minced onion
- 1 tsp garlic powder
- 15 oz. diced tomatoes with green chilies
- 15 oz. can diced tomatoes
- 15 oz. can pure pumpkin
- 15 oz. can red kidney beans
- 1 1/2 Tbsp chili powder
- 1/2 tsp cinnamon
- 2 cups beef broth
- Salt and pepper
- 1 cup hot water
- Side: veggies
- 1 gallon-size freezer baggie

Prepare to Freeze Instructions

- Brown ground beef with minced onion and garlic powder. Let cool.
- Open and drain can of diced tomatoes with green chiles, can of diced tomatoes, and can of red kidney beans. Rinse the beans. Open 2 cans of pumpkin.
- To gallon-size plastic freezer baggie in a round bowl/dish, add the following ingredients:
  - Ground beef
  - Tomatoes with green chiles
  - Diced tomatoes
  - Pumpkin
  - Red kidney beans
  - 1 1/2 Tbsp chili powder
  - 1/2 tsp cinnamon
    - Do NOT add beef broth to the freezer meal bag, add that at time of pressure cooking
- Remove as much air as possible and seal. Add label to baggie and freeze.

Cooking Directions

1. Open and drain the can of diced tomatoes with green chiles. Open the cans of diced tomatoes, pure pumpkin and red kidney beans. Rinse and drain the beans.
2. In a large saucepan, brown the ground beef with the minced onion and garlic powder. Drain and add to electric pressure cooker insert.
3. Note: You can skip the skillet and brown the ground beef using the Saute Mode of your Instant Pot. Tap on Saute, adjust to More/High, and brown the ground beef with the minced onion and garlic powder. Drain, if needed, and return the browned ground beef to the insert.
4. Stir in the diced tomatoes with green chiles, diced tomatoes, pure pumpkin, red kidney beans, chili powder and cinnamon with the ground beef. Season with salt and pepper to taste. Stir in the beef broth and hot water.
5. Steam valve: Sealing.
6. Cook on: Manual/High for 15 minutes.
7. Release: Natural or Quick.
8. Prepare veggies.
9. Serve Instant Pot Pumpkin Chili with veggies.

Freeze, Thaw & Pressure Cook Instructions

Put baggie in the freezer and freeze up to 6 months in fridge freezer or 12 months in a deep freezer. Thaw in the fridge overnight, or a bowl of warm water for about 20 minutes, before transferring to pressure cooker insert with 2 cups beef broth.

If cooking freezer meal from partially thawed, add the beef broth to the insert, add the frozen ingredients and adjust Pressure Cook time to 30 to 35 minutes.

Instant Pot Ranchero Chicken

Yield:	4 servings
Prep Time:	10 minutes
Cook Time:	15 minutes plus pressure build and release time

Ingredients

- 15 oz. can diced tomatoes
- 6 oz. can tomato paste
- 3 Tbsp taco seasoning
- 1 lb. boneless chicken breasts
- 1 lb. boneless chicken thighs
- 1/2 cup hot water
- Salt and pepper
- Side: rice
- Side: veggies
- 1 gallon-size freezer baggie

Prepare to Freeze Instructions

- Open can of diced tomatoes and tomato paste.
- To gallon-size plastic freezer baggie in a round bowl/dish, add the following ingredients:
  - Diced tomatoes
  - Tomato paste
  - 3 Tbsp taco seasoning
  - Chicken breasts
  - Chicken thighs
  - Salt and pepper
  - Do NOT add water to the freezer meal bag, add that at time of pressure cooking
- Remove as much air as possible and seal. Add label to baggie and freeze.

Cooking Directions

1. Whisk together the diced tomatoes with their juices and the tomato paste in the electric pressure cooker insert. Stir in the taco seasoning.
2. Add the chicken breast, thighs, and the hot water to the sauce in the electric pressure cooker insert. Spoon the sauce over the top.
3. Steam valve: Sealing.
4. Cook on: Manual/High for 15 minutes.
5. Release: Natural or Quick.
6. Once cooked, pull apart the chicken with 2 forks.
7. Cook rice, as directed.
8. Prepare veggies.
9. Serve Instant Pot Ranchero Chicken over rice with side of veggies.

Freeze, Thaw & Pressure Cook Instructions

Put baggie in the freezer and freeze up to 6 months in fridge freezer or 12 months in a deep freezer. Thaw in the fridge overnight, or a bowl of warm water for about 20 minutes, before adding contents of bag plus 1/2 cup hot water to electric pressure cooker insert. Pressure cook as directed.

If cooking freezer meal from partially thawed, add the hot water to the insert, add the frozen ingredients and adjust Pressure Cook time to 23 to 25 minutes.

Instant Pot Raspberry Chipotle Pork with Sweet Potatoes & Carrots

Yield:	4 servings
Prep Time:	10 minutes
Cook Time:	40 minutes plus pressure build and release time

Ingredients

- 2 lbs. pork roast
- 1/2 cup hot water
- 1 cup raspberry chipotle sauce
- Salt and pepper
- 4 medium sweet potatoes
- 1 lb. bag baby carrots
- Side: salad
- 1 gallon-size freezer baggie

Prepare to Freeze Instructions

- Peel and dice sweet potatoes. Place them in large bowl with water and soak them until you're ready to prepare the meal.
- To gallon-size plastic freezer baggie in a round bowl/dish, add the following ingredients:
  - Pork roast
  - Salt and pepper
  - Diced sweet potatoes
  - Baby carrots
  - 1 cup raspberry chipotle sauce
  - Do NOT add water to the freezer meal bag, add that at time of pressure cooking
- Remove as much air as possible and seal. Add label to baggie and freeze.

Cooking Directions

1. Peel and dice the sweet potatoes.
2. Add the pork roast to the electric pressure cooker insert with the hot water and sprinkle with salt and pepper. Pour the Raspberry Chipotle sauce over the top of pork.
3. Steam valve: Sealing.
4. Cook on: Manual/High for 40 minutes.
5. Release: Quick.
6. Open the lid and add the diced sweet potatoes and baby carrots around and on top of the pork roast. Put the lid back on and set valve to Sealing.
7. Cook on: Manual/High for 7 more minutes.
8. Release: Quick.
9. Prepare side salad.
10. Serve Instant Pot Raspberry Chipotle Pork Roast with Sweet Potatoes and Carrots and side salad.

Freeze, Thaw & Pressure Cook Instructions

Put baggie in the freezer and freeze up to 6 months in fridge freezer or 12 months in a deep freezer. Thaw in the fridge overnight, or a bowl of warm water for about 20 minutes, before adding contents of bag plus 1/2 cup hot water to electric pressure cooker insert. Pressure cook as directed.

If cooking freezer meal from partially thawed, add the hot water to the insert, add the frozen ingredients and adjust Pressure Cook time to 65 minutes.

Instant Pot Red Wine Beef Roast

Yield: 4 servings
Prep Time: 10 minutes
Cook Time: 55 minutes plus pressure build and release time

Ingredients

- 3 lbs. beef chuck roast
- Salt and pepper
- 1/4 cup red wine
- 1 cup beef broth
- 2 tsp minced garlic
- 2 tsp chopped chives
- 3 lbs. baby potatoes
- Side: salad
- 1 gallon-size freezer baggie

Prepare to Freeze Instructions

- To gallon-size plastic freezer baggie, add the following ingredients:
  - Beef roast
  - Salt and pepper
  - 1/4 cup red wine
  - 2 tsp minced garlic
  - 2 tsp chopped chives
  - Baby potatoes - add in separate baggie, if preferred
  - Do NOT add beef broth to the freezer meal bag, add that at time of pressure cooking
- Remove as much air as possible and seal. Add label to baggie and freeze.

Cooking Directions

1. Add the beef roast into the electric pressure cooker insert. Season with salt and pepper. Pour the red wine and beef broth around the beef roast. Sprinkle the minced garlic and chives right onto the beef roast. Do NOT add the baby potatoes at this time.
2. Steam valve: Sealing.
3. Cook on: Manual/High for 55 minutes.
4. Release: Quick.
5. Open the lid and add the baby potatoes around and on top of the beef roast. Put the lid back on and set valve to Sealing.
6. Cook on: Manual/High for 8 more minutes.
7. Release: Quick.
8. Quick release. Slice the beef. Make a gravy with flour or cornstarch, if desired.
9. Prepare the salad.
10. Serve Instant Red Wine Beef Roast and baby potatoes with side salad.

Freeze, Thaw & Pressure Cook Instructions

Put baggie in the freezer and freeze up to 6 months in fridge freezer or 12 months in a deep freezer. Thaw in the fridge overnight, or a bowl of warm water for about 20 minutes, before transferring only the beef roast and sauce into the electric pressure cooker insert. Pressure cook as directed, then add baby potatoes and finish cooking as directed.

If cooking freezer meal from partially thawed, add the hot water to the insert, add the frozen ingredients and adjust Pressure Cook time to 75 minutes.

Instant Pot Root Beer Pulled Pork

Yield: 4 servings
Prep Time: 10 minutes
Cook Time: 40 minutes plus pressure build and release time

Ingredients

- 2 lbs pork roast
- 1/2 cup hot water
- 1/2 small red onion
- Salt and pepper
- 12 oz. can root beer
- 16 oz. BBQ sauce
- 8 hamburger buns
- Side: Coleslaw salad kit
- Side: chips
- 1 gallon-size freezer baggie

Prepare to Freeze Instructions

- Thinly slice red onion.
- To gallon-size plastic freezer baggie in a round bowl/dish, add the following ingredients:
    - Pork roast
    - Red onion slices
    - Salt and pepper
    - 12 oz. can root beer
    - 16 oz. BBQ sauce
    - Do NOT add water to the freezer meal bag, add that at time of pressure cooking
- Remove as much air as possible and seal. Add label to baggie and freeze.

Cooking Directions

1. Thinly slice the red onion.
2. Place the pork roast and red onion slices into the electric pressure cooker insert with the hot water. Sprinkle with salt and pepper. Pour the root beer and BBQ sauce over the pork roast.
3. Steam valve: Sealing.
4. Cook on: Manual/High for 40 minutes.
5. Release: Natural or Quick.
6. Prepare the Coleslaw salad just before serving.
7. Once the pork roast is cooked, shred the meat with 2 forks and toss with the sauce. Spoon shredded pork onto hamburger buns and top with Coleslaw.
8. Serve Instant Pot Root Beer Pulled Pork with chips.

Freeze, Thaw & Pressure Cook Instructions

Put baggie in the freezer and freeze up to 6 months in fridge freezer or 12 months in a deep freezer. Thaw in the fridge overnight, or a bowl of warm water for about 20 minutes, before adding contents of bag plus 1/2 cup hot water to electric pressure cooker insert. Pressure cook as directed.

If cooking freezer meal from partially thawed, add the hot water to the insert, add the frozen ingredients and adjust Pressure Cook time to 65 minutes.

Instant Pot Russian Shredded Beef Sandwiches

Yield: 4 servings
Prep Time: 10 minutes
Cook Time: 50 minutes plus pressure build and release time

Ingredients

- 2 lbs. beef chuck roast
- 1/2 cup hot water
- Salt and pepper
- 1 cup Russian salad dressing
- 1 Tbsp minced onion
- 1 tsp garlic powder
- Salt and pepper
- Garnish: coleslaw
- 4 hoagie rolls
- Side: fruit
- 1 gallon-size freezer baggie

Prepare to Freeze Instructions

- To gallon-size plastic freezer baggie in a round bowl/dish, add the following ingredients:
  - Beef chuck roast
  - Salt and pepper
  - 1 cup Russian salad dressing
  - 1 Tbsp minced onion
  - 1 tsp garlic powder
  - Do NOT add water to the freezer meal bag, add that at time of pressure cooking
- Remove as much air as possible and seal. Add label to baggie and freeze.

Cooking Directions

1. Place the beef roast into the into the electric pressure cooker insert with the hot water. Season with salt and pepper. Pour the Russian salad dressing over the top and sprinkle the minced onion and garlic powder over the top.
2. Steam valve: Sealing.
3. Cook on: Manual/High for 50 minutes.
4. Release: Natural or Quick.
5. Once finished cooking, shred the beef with 2 forks and mix into the sauce.
6. Prepare the coleslaw, and assemble sandwiches with shredded beef and coleslaw.
7. Prepare the fruit.
8. Serve Instant Pot Russian Shredded Beef Sandwiches with side of fruit.

Freeze, Thaw & Pressure Cook Instructions

Put baggie in the freezer and freeze up to 6 months in fridge freezer or 12 months in a deep freezer. Thaw in the fridge overnight, or a bowl of warm water for about 20 minutes, before adding contents of bag plus 1/2 cup hot water to electric pressure cooker insert. Pressure cook as directed. Shred beef and prepare sandwiches as directed.

If cooking freezer meal from partially thawed, add the hot water to the insert, add the frozen ingredients and adjust Pressure Cook time to 75 minutes.

Instant Pot Salsa Beef Roast

Yield:	4 servings
Prep Time:	10 minutes
Cook Time:	60 minutes plus pressure build and release time

Ingredients

- 2 lbs. beef chuck roast
- 1/2 cup hot water
- 1 small white onion
- 2 cups salsa
- 1 Tbsp ground cumin
- Salt and pepper
- Side: rice
- Side: guacamole
- 1 gallon-size freezer baggie

Prepare to Freeze Instructions

- Slice the onion.
- To gallon-size plastic freezer baggie in a round bowl/dish, add the following ingredients:
  - Beef chuck roast
  - Onion
  - 2 cups salsa
  - 1 Tbsp ground cumin
  - Salt and pepper
  - Do NOT add water to the freezer meal bag, add that at time of pressure cooking
- Remove as much air as possible and seal. Add label to baggie and freeze.

Cooking Directions

1. Slice the onion.
2. Place the beef roast into the base of the electric pressure cooker insert with the hot water. Add the sliced onion, salsa, ground cumin and salt and pepper over the top of the beef roast.
3. Steam valve: Sealing.
4. Cook on: Manual/High for 60 minutes.
5. Release: Natural or Quick.
6. Once finished cooking, shred the beef and serve over rice.
7. Cook the rice, as directed.
8. Prepare the guacamole, if needed.
9. Serve Instant Pot Salsa Beef Roast over rice with guacamole.

Freeze, Thaw & Pressure Cook Instructions

Put baggie in the freezer and freeze up to 6 months in fridge freezer or 12 months in a deep freezer. Thaw in the fridge overnight, or a bowl of warm water for about 20 minutes, before adding contents of bag plus 1/2 cup hot water to electric pressure cooker insert. Pressure cook as directed.

If cooking freezer meal from partially thawed, add the hot water to the insert, add the frozen ingredients and adjust Pressure Cook time to 75 minutes.

Instant Pot Salsa Chicken

Yield:	4 servings
Prep Time:	10 minutes
Cook Time:	15 minutes plus pressure build and release time

Ingredients

- 2 large boneless chicken breasts
- 1/2 cup hot water
- 8 boneless chicken thighs
- 16 oz. red salsa
- 4 oz. can green chiles
- Salt and pepper
- Garnish: avocado slices
- Side: rice
- Side: veggies
- 1 gallon-size freezer baggie

Prepare to Freeze Instructions

- To gallon-size plastic freezer baggie in a round bowl/dish, add the following ingredients:
  - Chicken breasts
  - Chicken thighs
  - 16 oz. red salsa
  - 4 oz. can green chiles
  - Salt and pepper
  - Do NOT add water to the freezer meal bag, add that at time of pressure cooking
- Remove as much air as possible and seal. Add label to baggie and freeze.

Cooking Directions

1. Place the chicken breasts and chicken thighs in the base of the electric pressure cooker insert with the hot water and pour the red salsa and green chilies around the chicken. Season with salt and pepper.
2. Steam valve: Sealing.
3. Cook on: Manual/High for 15 minutes.
4. Release: Natural or Quick.
5. Once cooked, shred the chicken with 2 forks.
6. Cook the rice as directed.
7. Prepare veggies and slice avocado garnish.
8. Serve Instant Pot Salsa Chicken with avocado slices, over rice with veggies.

Freeze, Thaw & Pressure Cook Instructions

Put baggie in the freezer and freeze up to 6 months in fridge freezer or 12 months in a deep freezer. Thaw in the fridge overnight, or a bowl of warm water for about 20 minutes, before transferring to pressure cooker insert with 1/2 cup hot water. Pressure cook as directed.

If cooking freezer meal from partially thawed, add the hot water to the insert, add the frozen ingredients and adjust Pressure Cook time to 23 to 25 minutes.

Instant Pot Salsa Pork Chops

Yield:	4 servings
Prep Time:	10 minutes
Cook Time:	20 minutes plus pressure build and release time

Ingredients

- 4 boneless pork chops
- 1/2 cup hot water
- 8 oz. red salsa
- 4 oz. can green chiles
- Salt and pepper
- Garnish: avocado slices
- Side: rice
- Side: salad
- 1 gallon-size freezer baggie

Prepare to Freeze Instructions

- To gallon-size plastic freezer baggie in a round bowl/dish, add the following ingredients:
  - Pork chops
  - 8 oz. red salsa
  - 4 oz. can green chiles
  - Salt and pepper
  - Do NOT add water to the freezer meal bag, add that at time of pressure cooking
- Remove as much air as possible and seal. Add label to baggie and freeze.

Cooking Directions

1. Place the pork chops into the electric pressure cooker insert with the hot water.
2. Pour the red salsa and green chilies around the pork chops. Season with salt and pepper.
3. Steam valve: Sealing.
4. Cook on: Manual/High for 20 minutes.
5. Release: Natural or Quick.
6. Cook the rice as directed.
7. Prepare salad and slice avocado garnish.
8. Serve Instant Pot Salsa Pork Chops with avocado slices, over rice with veggies.

Freeze, Thaw & Pressure Cook Instructions

Put baggie in the freezer and freeze up to 6 months in fridge freezer or 12 months in a deep freezer. Thaw in the fridge overnight, or a bowl of warm water for about 20 minutes, before adding contents of bag plus 1/2 cup hot water to electric pressure cooker insert. Pressure cook as directed.

If cooking freezer meal from partially thawed, add the hot water to the insert, add the frozen ingredients and adjust Pressure Cook time to 24 minutes.

Instant Pot Salsa Verde Pork Tacos

Yield:	4 servings
Prep Time:	14 minutes
Cook Time:	40 minutes plus pressure build and release time

Ingredients

- 2 lbs. pork shoulder roast
- 1/2 cup hot water
- 1 tsp garlic powder
- 1 tsp ground cumin
- Salt and pepper
- 1 1/2 cups salsa verde sauce
- 1 large jalapeño
- 12 corn tortillas
- Garnish: crumbled goat cheese
- Garnish: sour cream
- Garnish: jalapeño
- Garnish: cilantro or avocado chunks
- Side: veggies
- 1 gallon-size freezer baggie

Prepare to Freeze Instructions

- Remove the seeds and dice jalapeño.
- To gallon-size plastic freezer baggie in a round bowl/dish, add the following ingredients:
  - Pork shoulder roast
  - 1 tsp garlic powder
  - 1 tsp ground cumin
  - Salt and pepper
  - 1 1/2 cups salsa verde sauce
  - 1 large jalapeño, diced
  - Do NOT add water to the freezer meal bag, add that at time of pressure cooking
- Remove as much air as possible and seal. Add label to baggie and freeze.

Cooking Directions

1. Dice the jalapeño.
2. Place the pork roast into the electric pressure cooker insert with the hot water. Sprinkle the garlic powder, ground cumin, salt and pepper on top of the pork roast. Pour the salsa verde and half of the diced jalapenos on top. Save the remaining jalapeño slices for garnish.
3. Steam valve: Sealing.
4. Cook on: Manual/High for 40 minutes.
5. Release: Natural or Quick.
6. Once the cooking time is complete, shred the pork with 2 forks and remove from the electric pressure cooker with slotted spoon when ready to serve. Spoon the shredded pork into the corn tortillas and add preferred toppings.
7. Prepare veggies.
8. Serve Instant Pot Salsa Verde Shredded Pork Tacos with veggies and preferred toppings.

Freeze, Thaw & Pressure Cook Instructions

Put baggie in the freezer and freeze up to 6 months in fridge freezer or 12 months in a deep freezer. Thaw in the fridge overnight, or a bowl of warm water for about 20 minutes, before adding contents of bag plus 1/2 cup hot water to electric pressure cooker insert. Pressure cook as directed.

If cooking freezer meal from partially thawed, add the hot water to the insert, add the frozen ingredients and adjust Pressure Cook time to 65 minutes.

Instant Pot Santa Fe Beef

Yield:	4 servings
Prep Time:	10 minutes
Cook Time:	60 minutes plus pressure build and release time

Ingredients

- 2 lbs. beef chuck roast
- 1/2 cup hot water
- Salt and pepper
- 1 packet taco seasoning
- 4 oz. can green chiles
- 1 cup red salsa
- Side: salad
- Side: dinner rolls
- 1 gallon-size freezer baggie

Prepare to Freeze Instructions

- Open can of green chiles.
- To gallon-size plastic freezer baggie in a round bowl/dish, add the following ingredients:
  - Beef chuck roast
  - Salt and pepper
  - 1 packet taco seasoning
  - 4 oz. can green chiles
  - 1 cup red salsa
  - Do NOT add water to the freezer meal bag, add that at time of pressure cooking
- Remove as much air as possible and seal. Add label to baggie and freeze.

Cooking Directions

1. Place the beef roast into the electric pressure cooker insert with the hot water. Season with salt and pepper. Sprinkle the taco seasoning over the roast. Pour the green chilies and red salsa over the top.
2. Steam valve: Sealing.
3. Cook on: Manual/High for 60 minutes.
4. Release: Natural or Quick.
5. Once finished cooking, shred the beef with 2 forks and mix into the sauce.
6. Prepare salad.
7. Warm the dinner rolls.
8. Serve Instant Pot Santa Fe Beef with salad and dinner rolls.

Freeze, Thaw & Pressure Cook Instructions

Put baggie in the freezer and freeze up to 6 months in fridge freezer or 12 months in a deep freezer. Thaw in the fridge overnight, or a bowl of warm water for about 20 minutes, before adding contents of bag plus 1/2 cup hot water to electric pressure cooker insert. Pressure cook as directed.

If cooking freezer meal from partially thawed, add the hot water to the insert, add the frozen ingredients and adjust Pressure Cook time to 75 minutes.

Instant Pot Santa Fe Chicken

Yield:	4 servings
Prep Time:	10 minutes
Cook Time:	15 minutes plus pressure build and release time

Ingredients

- 4 small boneless chicken breasts
- 1 cup hot water
- 15 oz. can black beans
- 15 oz. can corn
- 1 cup red salsa
- 1 tsp garlic powder
- 1 tsp ground cumin
- Salt and pepper
- 4 oz. cream cheese
- 8 flour tortillas
- Garnish: cilantro
- Side: veggies
- 1 gallon-size freezer baggie

Prepare to Freeze Instructions

- Open and drain can of corn.
- Open, drain and rinse can of black beans.
- To gallon-size plastic freezer baggie in a round bowl/dish, add the following ingredients:
  - Black beans
  - Corn
  - 1 cup red salsa
  - 1 tsp garlic powder
  - 1 tsp ground cumin
  - Do NOT add the water or cream cheese before freezing.
- Remove as much air as possible and seal. Add label to baggie and freeze.

Cooking Directions

1. Open, drain and rinse the black beans.
2. Open and drain the corn.
3. 3. Place the chicken breasts in the electric pressure cooker insert with the hot water. Pour the black beans, corn, salsa, garlic powder and ground cumin over the top.
4. Steam valve: Sealing.
5. Cook on: Manual/High for 15 minutes.
6. Release: Natural or Quick.
7. After cooking, shred the chicken with forks and stir the cream cheese into the sauce. Cook for 30 more minutes to allow sauce to thicken. Stir again before serving. Season with salt and pepper to taste.
8. Prepare veggies.
9. Serve Instant Pot Santa Fe Chicken in tortillas with cilantro garnish and side of veggies.

Freeze, Thaw & Pressure Cook Instructions

Put baggie in the freezer and freeze up to 6 months in fridge freezer or 12 months in a deep freezer. Thaw in the fridge overnight, or a bowl of warm water for about 20 minutes, before adding contents of bag plus 1 cup hot water to electric pressure cooker insert. Pressure cook as directed.

If cooking freezer meal from partially thawed, add the hot water to the insert, add the frozen ingredients and adjust Pressure Cook time to 23 to 25 minutes.

Instant Pot Shredded Beef Tacos with Mango Avocado Salsa

Yield:	4 servings
Prep Time:	10 minutes
Cook Time:	60 minutes plus pressure build and release time

Ingredients

- 1 1/2 lbs. beef roast
- 1 cup hot water
- 1 lime
- 1 tsp ground cumin
- Salt and pepper
- 1 mango
- 1 lime
- 2 small avocados
- 1 small bunch cilantro
- 12 tortillas, flour or corn
- Side: corn on the cob
- 1 gallon-size freezer baggie

Prepare to Freeze Instructions

- Halve lime.
- To gallon-size plastic freezer baggie in a round bowl/dish, add the following ingredients:
  - Beef roast
  - Lime Juice
  - 1 tsp ground cumin
  - Salt and pepper
  - Note: Do NOT add the water or fresh produce for the mango salsa or tortillas to the freezer baggies.
- Remove as much air as possible and seal. Add label to baggie and freeze.

Cooking Directions

1. Place the beef roast into the pressure cooker insert with the hot water. Squeeze juice from one lime over the top, then sprinkle with cumin, salt and pepper.
2. Steam valve: Sealing.
3. Cook on: Manual/High for 60 minutes.
4. Release: Natural or Quick.
5. Once cooked, shred it with 2 forks.
6. Before dinner, mix up the diced mango, diced avocado, juice from remaining lime, cilantro and salt and pepper together in a bowl.
7. Add the slow cooked beef into the tortillas and top with the mango-avocado salsa.
8. Prepare corn on the cob.
9. Serve Instant Pot Shredded Beef Tacos with Mango Avocado Salsa and corn on the cob.

Freeze, Thaw & Pressure Cook Instructions

Put baggie in the freezer and freeze up to 6 months in fridge freezer or 12 months in a deep freezer. Thaw in the fridge overnight, or a bowl of warm water for about 20 minutes, before adding contents of bag plus 1 cup hot water to electric pressure cooker insert. Pressure cook as directed.

If cooking freezer meal from partially thawed, add the hot water to the insert, add the frozen ingredients and adjust Pressure Cook time to 75 minutes.

Instant Pot Shredded Hawaiian Chicken Sandwiches

Yield: 4 servings
Prep Time: 10 minutes
Cook Time: 15 minutes plus pressure build and release time

Ingredients

- 3 large boneless chicken breasts
- 1/2 cup hot water
- Salt and pepper
- 1/2 cup BBQ sauce
- 20 oz. can crushed pineapple
- 1 small red onion
- 8 hamburger buns
- Side: chips
- 1 gallon-size freezer baggie

Prepare to Freeze Instructions

- Finely chop red onion.
- Open can of crushed pineapple. Do not drain.
- To gallon-size plastic freezer baggie in a round bowl/dish, add the following ingredients:
  - Chicken breasts
  - Salt and pepper
  - 1/2 cup BBQ sauce
  - Canned pineapple, undrained
  - Chopped red onion
  - Do NOT add water to the freezer meal bag, add that at time of pressure cooking
- Remove as much air as possible and seal. Add label to baggie and freeze.

Cooking Directions

1. Chop the red onion.
2. Place the chicken breasts into the electric pressure cooker insert with the hot water. Sprinkle a little salt and pepper over the top. Drizzle BBQ sauce over the chicken breasts and then pour the pineapple juices around the chicken breasts and the pineapple and chopped red onion on top of the chicken.
3. Steam valve: Sealing.
4. Cook on: Manual/High for 15 minutes.
5. Release: Natural.
6. Once cooked, pull out the chicken breasts and the pineapple and add to a bowl, then shred with 2 forks. Mix in the chopped red onion, if you didn't add it to the pressure cooker. Add shredded chicken and sauce to sandwich buns.
7. Prepare fruit, as needed.
8. Serve Instant Pot Shredded Hawaiian Chicken Sandwiches with fruit and chips.

Freeze, Thaw & Pressure Cook Instructions

Put baggie in the freezer and freeze up to 6 months in fridge freezer or 12 months in a deep freezer. Thaw in the fridge overnight, or a bowl of warm water for about 20 minutes, before adding contents of bag plus 1/2 cup hot water to electric pressure cooker insert. Pressure cook as directed.

If cooking freezer meal from partially thawed, add the hot water to the insert, add the frozen ingredients and adjust Pressure Cook time to 23 to 25 minutes.

Instant Pot Shredded Italian Beef Hoagies

Yield:	4 servings
Prep Time:	10 minutes
Cook Time:	50 minutes plus pressure build and release time

Ingredients

- 2 lbs. beef chuck roast
- 1/2 cup hot water
- Salt and pepper
- 15 oz. can crushed tomatoes
- 2 Tbsp Italian seasoning
- 1 Tbsp balsamic vinegar
- 4 hoagie rolls
- 8 slices Provolone cheese
- Side: salad
- 1 gallon-size freezer baggie

Prepare to Freeze Instructions

- Open crushed tomatoes.
- To gallon-size plastic freezer baggie in a round bowl/dish, add the following ingredients:
  - Beef chuck roast
  - Salt and pepper
  - Crushed tomatoes
  - 2 Tbsp Italian seasoning
  - 1 Tbsp balsamic vinegar
  - Do NOT add water to the freezer meal bag, add that at time of pressure cooking
- Remove as much air as possible and seal. Add label to baggie and freeze.

Cooking Directions

1. Place the beef roast into the base of the electric pressure cooker insert with the hot water and season with salt and pepper. Add the crushed tomatoes onto the roast and then sprinkle the Italian seasoning and balsamic vinegar over the top.
2. Steam valve: Sealing.
3. Cook on: Manual/High for 50 minutes.
4. Release: Natural or Quick.
5. Once finished cooking, shred the beef with 2 forks and mix into the sauce.
6. Assemble the hoagies with shredded beef, sauce and slices of Provolone cheese. If preferred, place under the oven broiler to melt the cheese.
7. Prepare salad.
8. Serve Instant Pot Shredded Italian Beef Hoagies with salad.

Freeze, Thaw & Pressure Cook Instructions

Put baggie in the freezer and freeze up to 6 months in fridge freezer or 12 months in a deep freezer. Thaw in the fridge overnight, or a bowl of warm water for about 20 minutes, before transferring to pressure cooker insert with 1/2 cup hot water. Pressure cook as directed.

If cooking freezer meal from partially thawed, add the hot water to the insert, add the frozen ingredients and adjust Pressure Cook time to 75 minutes.

Instant Pot Shredded Pork with Thai Peanut Sauce

Yield: 4 servings
Prep Time: 10 minutes
Cook Time: 40 minutes plus pressure build and release time

Ingredients

- 2 lbs. pork roast
- 1/2 cup hot water
- Salt and pepper
- 1 red bell pepper
- 1 small white onion
- 1/2 cup soy sauce
- 1/4 cup peanut butter
- 1 Tbsp vinegar
- 1 Tbsp lime juice
- 1 tsp ground ginger
- 1 tsp garlic powder
- Garnish: green onions and lime slices
- Garnish: chopped peanuts
- Side: rice
- Side: salad
- 1 gallon-size freezer baggie

Prepare to Freeze Instructions

- Seed and slice red bell pepper. Thinly slice onion.
- In a mixing bowl, whisk together soy sauce, peanut butter, vinegar, lime juice, ground ginger and garlic powder. Add in a few pinches of salt and pepper.
- To gallon-size plastic freezer baggie in a round bowl/dish, add the following ingredients:
  - Pork roast
  - Sliced red bell peppers
  - Sliced onions
  - Salt and pepper
  - Prepared sauce
  - Do NOT add water to the freezer meal bag, add that at time of pressure cooking
- Remove as much air as possible and seal. Add label to baggie and freeze.

Cooking Directions

1. Seed and slice the red bell pepper. Thinly slice the onion.
2. In a mixing bowl, whisk together the soy sauce, peanut butter, vinegar, lime juice, ground ginger and garlic powder. Add in a few pinches of salt and pepper.
3. Add the pork roast to the electric pressure cooker insert with the hot water. Add the bell peppers and onions over the top. Pour the Thai peanut sauce over the top.
4. Steam valve: Sealing.
5. Cook on: Manual/High for 40 minutes.
6. Release: Natural or Quick.
7. Once cooked, use 2 forks and shred the pork meat into the sauce.
8. Cook rice, as directed.
9. Prepare salad.
10. Serve Instant Pot Shredded Pork with Thai Peanut Sauce over rice with side salad.

Freeze, Thaw & Pressure Cook Instructions

Put baggie in the freezer and freeze up to 6 months in fridge freezer or 12 months in a deep freezer. Thaw in the fridge overnight, or a bowl of warm water for about 20 minutes, before adding contents of bag plus 1/2 cup hot water to electric pressure cooker insert. Pressure cook as directed.

If cooking freezer meal from partially thawed, add the hot water to the insert, add the frozen ingredients and adjust Pressure Cook time to 65 minutes.

Instant Pot Slopp-Beany Joes

Yield:	4 servings
Prep Time:	10 minutes
Cook Time:	15 minutes plus pressure build and release time

Ingredients

- 1 lb. ground beef
- 2 - 15 oz. cans white beans
- 2 - 15 oz. cans sloppy joe sauce
- Salt and pepper
- 8 sandwich buns
- 1 cup hot water
- Side: salad
- 1 gallon-size freezer baggie

Prepare to Freeze Instructions

- Brown ground beef and drain well. Set aside and let cool.
- Open, drain and rinse can white beans. Open can sloppy joe sauce.
- To gallon-size plastic freezer baggie in a round bowl/dish, add the following ingredients:
  - Browned ground beef
  - Small white beans
  - Sloppy joe sauce
  - Do NOT add water to the freezer meal bag, add that at time of pressure cooking
- Remove as much as air as possible and seal.

Cooking Directions

1. Open, drain and rinse can white beans. Open can sloppy joe sauce.
2. In a large skillet, brown the ground beef. Drain and add the browned ground beef to the pressure cooker insert.
3. Note: You can skip the skillet and brown the ground beef using the Saute Mode of your Instant Pot. Tap on Saute, adjust to More/High, and brown the ground beef. Drain, if needed, and return the browned ground beef to the insert
4. Stir in the white beans, sloppy joe sauce, plus hot water into the electric pressure cooker insert.
5. Steam valve: Sealing.
6. Cook on: Manual/High for 15 minutes.
7. Release: Natural or Quick.
8. Prepare salad.
9. Assemble sandwiches.
10. Serve Slopp-Beany Joes with salad.

Freeze, Thaw & Pressure Cook Instructions

Put baggie in the freezer and freeze up to 6 months in fridge freezer or 12 months in a deep freezer. Thaw in the fridge overnight, or a bowl of warm water for about 20 minutes, before transferring to pressure cooker insert with 1 cup hot water.

If cooking freezer meal from partially thawed, add the hot water to the insert, add the frozen ingredients and adjust Pressure Cook time to 30 to 35 minutes.

Instant Pot Sloppy Shredded Beef Sandwiches

Yield: 4 servings
Prep Time: 10 minutes
Cook Time: 40 minutes plus pressure build and release time

Ingredients

- 2 lbs beef chuck roast
- 1/2 cup hot water
- Salt and pepper
- 1 small white onion
- 15 oz. can diced tomatoes
- 15 oz. can sloppy joe sauce
- 8 hamburger buns
- Side: salad
- Side: fruit
- 1 gallon-size freezer baggie

Prepare to Freeze Instructions

- Slice white onion into half moons.
- Open and drain can of diced tomatoes. Open can of sloppy joe sauce.
- To gallon-size plastic freezer baggie in a round bowl/dish, add the following ingredients:
  - Beef chuck roast
  - Salt and pepper
  - Sliced onions
  - Drained diced tomatoes
  - Sloppy joe sauce
  - Do NOT add water to the freezer meal bag, add that at time of pressure cooking
- Remove as much air as possible and seal. Add label to baggie and freeze.

Cooking Directions

1. Slice the onion into half moons.
2. Open and drain the diced tomatoes. Open the sloppy joe sauce.
3. Place the beef roast into the electric pressure cooker insert with the hot water and season with salt and pepper. Sprinkle the sliced onions over the top, then pour the diced tomatoes and sloppy joe sauce over the top.
4. Steam valve: Sealing.
5. Cook on: Manual/High for 40 minutes.
6. Release: Natural or Quick.
7. Once finished cooking, shred the beef with 2 forks and mix into the sauce. Assemble sandwiches with hamburger buns and meat sauce.
8. Prepare salad and fruit.
9. Serve Instant Pot Sloppy Shredded Beef Sandwiches with salad and fruit.

Freeze, Thaw & Pressure Cook Instructions

Put baggie in the freezer and freeze up to 6 months in fridge freezer or 12 months in a deep freezer. Thaw in the fridge overnight, or a bowl of warm water for about 20 minutes, before adding contents of bag plus 1/2 cup hot water to electric pressure cooker insert. Pressure cook as directed.

If cooking freezer meal from partially thawed, add the hot water to the insert, add the frozen ingredients and adjust Pressure Cook time to 75 minutes.

Instant Pot Southwestern Pork Roast

Yield:	4 servings
Prep Time:	10 minutes
Cook Time:	40 minutes plus pressure build and release time

Ingredients

- 2 lbs. pork roast
- 1/2 cup hot water
- Salt and pepper
- 2 Tbsp brown sugar
- 2 Tbsp minced onion
- 1 Tbsp chili powder
- 1 Tbsp ground cumin
- 2 - 4 oz. cans green chiles
- Side: dinner rolls
- Side: salad
- 1 gallon-size freezer baggie

Prepare to Freeze Instructions

- In a small mixing bowl, combine brown sugar, minced onion, chili powder and ground cumin.
- Open cans of green chilies.
- To gallon-size plastic freezer baggie in a round bowl/dish, add the following ingredients:
  - Pork roast
  - Salt and pepper
  - Spice mixture
  - Canned green chilies
  - Do NOT add water to the freezer meal bag, add that at time of pressure cooking
- Remove as much air as possible and seal. Add label to baggie and freeze.

Cooking Directions

1. In a small mixing bowl, combine the brown sugar, minced onion, chili powder and ground cumin.
2. Place the pork roast into the electric pressure cooker insert with the hot water. Season with salt and pepper. Then add the spice mixture directly onto the pork. Top with cans of green chilies onto the pork roast.
3. Steam valve: Sealing.
4. Cook on: Manual/High for 40 minutes.
5. Release: Natural or Quick.
6. Warm the dinner rolls.
7. Prepare the salad.
8. Serve Instant Pot Southwestern Pork Roast with dinner rolls and salad.

Freeze, Thaw & Pressure Cook Instructions

Put baggie in the freezer and freeze up to 6 months in fridge freezer or 12 months in a deep freezer. Thaw in the fridge overnight, or a bowl of warm water for about 20 minutes, before adding contents of bag plus 1/2 cup hot water to electric pressure cooker insert. Pressure cook as directed.

If cooking freezer meal from partially thawed, add the hot water to the insert, add the frozen ingredients and adjust Pressure Cook time to 65 minutes.

Instant Pot Spicy Mango Chicken Tacos

Yield: 4 servings
Prep Time: 10 minutes
Cook Time: 15 minutes plus pressure build and release time

Ingredients

- 2 large boneless chicken breasts
- 4 boneless chicken thighs
- 1/2 cup hot water
- 1 cup mango nectar
- 1 Tbsp ground cumin
- 1/2 cup salsa
- 15 oz. can black beans
- 4 oz. can green chiles
- Salt and pepper
- 8 flour tortillas
- Side: avocados
- 1 gallon-size freezer baggie

Prepare to Freeze Instructions

- Open, drain and rinse can of black beans.
- Open can of green chiles.
- To gallon-size plastic freezer baggie in a round bowl/dish, add the following ingredients:
  - Chicken breasts
  - Chicken thighs
  - 1 cup mango nectar
  - 1 Tbsp ground cumin
  - 1/2 cup salsa
  - Drained and rinsed black beans
  - Canned green chiles
  - Salt and pepper
  - Do NOT add water to the freezer meal bag, add that at time of pressure cooking
- Remove as much air as possible and seal. Add label to baggie and freeze.

Cooking Directions

1. Open, drain, and rinse the black beans.
2. Place the chicken breasts and chicken thighs into the electric pressure cooker insert with the hot water. Add the mango nectar, ground cumin, salsa, drained black beans, green chiles, salt and pepper on top of the chicken.
3. Steam valve: Sealing.
4. Cook on: Manual/High for 15 minutes.
5. Release: Natural or Quick.
6. Once finished cooking, shred the chicken with 2 forks and mix into the sauce with the black beans.
7. Spoon the shredded chicken into tortillas and make tacos.
8. Prepare avocado.
9. Serve Instant Pot Spicy Mango Chicken Tacos with avocado.

Freeze, Thaw & Pressure Cook Instructions

Put baggie in the freezer and freeze up to 6 months in fridge freezer or 12 months in a deep freezer. Thaw in the fridge overnight, or a bowl of warm water for about 20 minutes, before adding contents of bag plus 1/2 cup hot water to electric pressure cooker insert. Pressure cook as directed.

If cooking freezer meal from partially thawed, add the hot water to the insert, add the frozen ingredients and adjust Pressure Cook time to 23 to 25 minutes.

Instant Pot Sweet Chili Pork Chops

Yield:	4 servings
Prep Time:	5 minutes
Cook Time:	20 minutes plus pressure build and release time

Ingredients

- 4 boneless pork chops
- 1 cup hot water
- Salt and pepper
- 1/4 cup sweet Thai chili sauce
- Side: rice
- Side: veggies
- 1 gallon-size freezer baggie

Prepare to Freeze Instructions

- To gallon-size plastic freezer baggie in a round bowl/dish, add the following ingredients:
  - Pork chops
  - Salt and pepper
  - 1/4 cup sweet Thai chili sauce
  - Do NOT add water to the freezer meal bag, add that at time of pressure cooking
- Remove as much air as possible, add label and freeze.

Cooking Directions

1. Pour the water into the base of the insert. Add a steamer rack and place the pork chops on the rack and season with salt and pepper. Brush the sweet Thai chili sauce onto each pork chop.
2. Steam valve: Sealing.
3. Cook on: Manual/High for 20 minutes.
4. Release: Natural or Quick.
5. Let rest for 5 minutes before serving or slicing. Cooking time may vary depending on thickness of the pork chops.
6. Cook the rice, as directed.
7. Prepare veggies.
8. Serve Instant Pot Sweet Chili Pork Chops with veggies and rice.

Freeze, Thaw & Pressure Cook Instructions

Put baggie in the freezer and freeze up to 6 months in fridge freezer or 12 months in a deep freezer. Thaw in the fridge overnight, or a bowl of warm water for about 20 minutes, before transferring to pressure cooker insert with 1 cup hot water. Pressure cook as directed.

If cooking freezer meal from partially thawed, add the hot water to the insert, add the frozen ingredients and adjust Pressure Cook time to 24 minutes.

Instant Pot Taco Soup

Yield:	4 servings
Prep Time:	15 minutes
Cook Time:	15 minutes plus pressure build and release time

Ingredients

- 1 lb. ground beef
- 15 oz. can black beans
- 15 oz. can diced tomatoes
- 15 oz. can corn
- 2 Tbsp chili powder
- 1 tsp ground cumin
- 1 tsp garlic powder
- 1 tsp onion powder
- Salt and pepper
- 2 cups chicken broth
- 1 cup hot water
- Garnish: corn tortilla chips
- Garnish: shredded cheese
- Side: veggies
- 1 gallon-size freezer baggie

Prepare to Freeze Instructions

- Brown and drain ground beef.
- Open, drain and rinse can of black beans.
- Open can of diced tomatoes.
- Open and drain can of corn.
- To gallon-size plastic freezer baggie in a round bowl/dish, add the following ingredients:
  - Browned ground beef
  - Black beans, drained and rinsed
  - Diced tomatoes, undrained
  - Corn, drained
  - 2 Tbsp chili powder
  - 1 tsp ground cumin
  - 1 tsp garlic powder
  - 1 tsp onion powder
  - Do NOT add chicken broth to the freezer meal bag, add that at time of pressure cooking
- Remove as much air as possible and seal. Add label to baggie and freeze.

Cooking Directions

1. Open the can of diced tomatoes. Open, drain and rinse the black beans. Open and drain the corn.
2. In a large saucepan, brown and drain the ground beef. Drain and add the browned ground beef to the pressure cooker insert.
3. Note: You can skip the skillet and brown the ground beef using the Saute Mode of your Instant Pot. Tap on Saute, adjust to More/High, and brown the ground beef. Drain, if needed, and return the browned ground beef to the insert.
4. Add the black beans, corn, diced tomatoes, and chicken broth into the electric pressure cooker insert.
5. Stir in the chili powder, ground cumin, garlic powder, onion powder and hot water in with the other ingredients.
6. Steam valve: Sealing.
7. Cook on: Manual/High for 15 minutes.
8. Release: Natural or Quick.
9. Serve Instant Pot Taco Soup, with crushed tortilla chips and cheese as garnish, with a side of veggies.

Freeze, Thaw & Pressure Cook Instructions

Put baggie in the freezer and freeze up to 6 months in fridge freezer or 12 months in a deep freezer. Thaw in the fridge overnight, or a bowl of warm water for about 20 minutes, before transferring to pressure cooker insert with 2 cups chicken broth. Pressure cook as directed.

If cooking freezer meal from partially thawed, add the hot water to the insert, add the frozen ingredients and adjust Pressure Cook time to 23 to 25 minutes.

Instant Pot Teriyaki Pork Tenderloin

Yield: 4 servings
Prep Time: 10 minutes
Cook Time: 40 minutes plus pressure build and release time

Ingredients

- 2 lbs. pork tenderloin
- 1/2 cup hot water
- 1 small white onion
- 1 cup teriyaki sauce
- 2 tsp minced garlic
- 1 tsp crushed red pepper flakes
- Salt and pepper
- Garnish: sliced green onions
- Side: rice
- Side: veggies
- 1 gallon-size freezer baggie

Prepare to Freeze Instructions

- Thinly slice onion.
- To gallon-size plastic freezer baggie in a round bowl/dish, add the following ingredients:
  - Pork tenderloin
  - Sliced white onions
  - 1 cup teriyaki sauce
  - 2 tsp minced garlic
  - 1 tsp crushed red pepper flakes
  - Salt and pepper
  - Do NOT add water to the freezer meal bag, add that at time of pressure cooking
- Remove as much air as possible and seal. Add label to baggie and freeze.

Cooking Directions

1. Thinly slice the onion.
2. Add the pork tenderloin to the electric pressure cooker insert with the hot water. Add the thin onion slices on top. Pour the teriyaki sauce onto the pork tenderloin and onion slices. Add the minced garlic and crushed red pepper flakes over the top. Sprinkle salt and pepper to taste.
3. Steam valve: Sealing.
4. Cook on: Manual/High for 40 minutes.
5. Release: Natural or Quick.
6. Remove tenderloin and let sit for 5 minutes before slicing. Spoon sauce over sliced pork pieces.
7. Cook the rice, as directed.
8. Prepare veggies.
9. Serve Instant Pot Teriyaki Pork Tenderloin with sliced green onions garnish, rice and veggies.

Freeze, Thaw & Pressure Cook Instructions

Put baggie in the freezer and freeze up to 6 months in fridge freezer or 12 months in a deep freezer. Thaw in the fridge overnight, or a bowl of warm water for about 20 minutes, before adding contents of bag plus 1/2 cup hot water to electric pressure cooker insert. Pressure cook as directed.

If cooking freezer meal from partially thawed, add the hot water to the insert, add the frozen ingredients and adjust Pressure Cook time to 65 minutes.

Instant Pot Thai Peanut Chicken

Yield:	4 servings
Prep Time:	10 minutes
Cook Time:	15 minutes plus pressure build and release time

Ingredients

- 4 small boneless chicken breasts
- Salt and pepper
- 1/4 cup hot water
- 1 small white onion
- 1 red bell pepper
- 1 cup Thai peanut sauce
- Garnish: sesame seeds and green onions
- Garnish: chopped peanuts
- Side: rice
- Side: veggies
- 1 gallon-size freezer baggie

Prepare to Freeze Instructions

- Dice small white onion.
- Seed and dice red bell pepper.
- To gallon-size plastic freezer baggie in a round bowl/dish, add the following ingredients:
  - Chicken breasts
  - Salt and pepper
  - Diced onion
  - Diced bell peppers
  - 1 cup Thai peanut sauce
  - Do NOT add water to the freezer meal bag, add that at time of pressure cooking
- Remove as much air as possible and seal. Add label to baggie and freeze.

Cooking Directions

1. Dice the white onion. Seed and dice the red bell pepper.
2. Place the chicken into the electric pressure cooker insert with the hot water. Season with salt and pepper.
3. Add the diced onions and red bell peppers, then pour the Thai peanut sauce over the top.
4. Steam valve: Sealing.
5. Release: Natural or Quick.
6. Cook on: Manual/High for 15 minutes.
7. Cook the rice as directed.
8. Prepare the veggies and garnishes.
9. Serve Instant Pot Thai Peanut Chicken over rice with garnishes and a side of veggies.

Freeze, Thaw & Pressure Cook Instructions

Put baggie in the freezer and freeze up to 6 months in fridge freezer or 12 months in a deep freezer. Thaw in the fridge overnight, or a bowl of warm water for about 20 minutes, before adding contents of bag plus 1/4 cup hot water to electric pressure cooker insert. Pressure cook as directed.

If cooking freezer meal from partially thawed, add the hot water to the insert, add the frozen ingredients and adjust Pressure Cook time to 23 to 25 minutes.

Instant Pot Tuscan Ham & Bean Soup

Yield: 4 servings
Prep Time: 15 minutes
Cook Time: 15 minutes plus pressure build and release time

Ingredients

- 2 cups chopped ham
- 1 small white onion
- 4 whole carrots
- 1 tsp minced garlic
- 15 oz. can Cannellini beans
- 15 oz. can red kidney beans
- 4 cups vegetable stock
- 10 oz. box frozen spinach
- 1 tsp dried basil
- 1 tsp dried thyme
- Salt and pepper
- Garnish: shredded Parmesan cheese
- Side: loaf bread
- 1 gallon-size freezer baggie

Prepare to Freeze Instructions

- Partially thaw box of frozen spinach.
- Chop white onion. Peel and chop whole carrots.
- Open and drain can of red kidney beans and the can of cannellini beans.
- To gallon-size plastic freezer baggie in a round bowl/dish, add the following ingredients:
  - Chopped ham
  - Chopped onion
  - Chopped carrots
  - 1 tsp minced garlic
  - Cannellini beans, drained
  - Red kidney beans, drained
  - Frozen spinach
  - 1 tsp dried basil
  - 1 tsp dried thyme
  - Salt and pepper
  - Do NOT add vegetable stock to the freezer meal bag, add that at time of pressure cooking
- Remove as much air as possible and seal. Add label to baggie and freeze.

Cooking Directions

1. Chop the white onion. Peel and chop the carrots.
2. Open and drain the cans of beans.
3. Thaw the frozen spinach.
4. Add all ingredients except the garnish and side dish to the electric pressure cooker insert.
5. Steam valve: Sealing.
6. Cook on: Manual/High for 15 minutes.
7. Release: Natural or Quick.
8. Warm the loaf bread.
9. Serve Instant Pot Tuscan Ham & Bean Soup with warm loaf bread and butter.

Freeze, Thaw & Pressure Cook Instructions

Put baggie in the freezer and freeze up to 6 months in fridge freezer or 12 months in a deep freezer. Thaw in the fridge overnight, or a bowl of warm water for about 20 minutes, before transferring to pressure cooker insert with 4 cups vegetable stock. Pressure cook as directed.

If cooking freezer meal from partially thawed, add the vegetable stock to the insert, add the frozen ingredients and adjust Pressure Cook time to 30 to 35 minutes.

Instant Pot White Wine Artichoke Chicken

Yield: 4 servings
Prep Time: 10 minutes
Cook Time: 15 minutes plus pressure build and release time

Ingredients

- 4 small boneless chicken breasts
- 1 cup hot water
- 1 cup white cooking wine
- 1 cup chicken stock
- 15 oz. can artichoke hearts
- 2 Tbsp butter
- 1 Tbsp lemon juice
- Salt and pepper
- 1 Tbsp cornstarch
- Side: pasta
- Side: salad
- 1 gallon-size freezer baggie

Prepare to Freeze Instructions

- Open and drain the can of artichoke hearts.
- To gallon-size plastic freezer baggie in a round bowl/dish, add the following ingredients:
  - Chicken breasts
  - 1 cup white cooking wine
  - Canned artichoke hearts
  - 2 Tbsp butter
  - 1 Tbsp lemon juice
  - Salt and pepper
  - Do NOT add chicken stock or cornstarch to the freezer bag , add that at time of pressure cooking
- Remove as much air as possible and seal. Add label to baggie and freeze.

Cooking Directions

1. Open and drain the can of artichokes.
2. Place the chicken breasts into the electric pressure cooker insert with the hot water.
3. Pour the white wine, chicken stock, artichoke hearts, butter, and lemon juice around the chicken. Season with salt and pepper.
4. Steam valve: Sealing.
5. Cook on: Manual/High for 15 minutes.
6. Release: Natural or Quick.
7. Whisk in the cornstarch. The sauce will thicken.
8. Cook the pasta as directed.
9. Prepare salad.
10. Serve Instant Pot White Wine Artichoke Chicken over pasta with salad.

Freeze, Thaw & Pressure Cook Instructions

Put baggie in the freezer and freeze up to 6 months in fridge freezer or 12 months in a deep freezer. Thaw in the fridge overnight, or a bowl of warm water for about 20 minutes, before adding contents of bag plus 1 cup hot water to electric pressure cooker insert. Pressure cook as directed.

If cooking freezer meal from partially thawed, add the chicken stock to the insert, add the frozen ingredients and adjust Pressure Cook time to 23 to 25 minutes.

Instant Pot Adobo Pulled Pork Sandwiches

Yield: 4 servings
Prep Time: 10 minutes
Cook Time: 50 minutes plus pressure build and release time

Ingredients

- 2 Tbsp olive oil
- 2 lbs. pork roast
- Salt and pepper, to taste
- 8 oz. can tomato sauce
- 2 Tbsp brown sugar
- 1 tsp garlic powder
- 1 tsp chili powder
- 1 Tbsp Adobo seasoning
- 1 cup water
- 8 hamburger buns
- Side: veggies
- Side: chips

Prepare to Freeze Instructions

- Open the tomato sauce.
- To gallon-size plastic freezer baggie in a round bowl/dish, add the following ingredients:
  - 2 lbs. pork roast
  - Salt and pepper
  - Can of tomato sauce
  - 2 Tbsp brown sugar
  - 1 tsp garlic powder
  - 1 tsp chili powder
  - 1 Tbsp Adobo seasoning
  - Do NOT add water to the freezer meal bag, add that at time of pressure cooking
- Remove as much air as possible and seal. Add label to baggie and freeze.

Cooking Directions

1. In a small bowl, combine the tomato sauce, brown sugar, garlic powder, chili powder and Adobo seasoning.
2. Turn the Instant Pot on Saute mode and add the olive oil and brown all sides of the pork roast. Once browned, tap Cancel.
3. Then add 1 cup water around the pork roast and pour the tomato sauce mixture over the pork.
4. Steam valve: Sealing.
5. Cook on: Manual/High for 50 minutes.
6. Release: Natural or Quick.
7. Shred the pork into the juices and strain, if needed.
8. Spoon the shredded pork onto buns.
9. Prepare the veggies.
10. Serve Instant Pot Adobo Pulled Pork Sandwiches with veggies and chips.

Freeze, Thaw & Pressure Cook Instructions

Put baggie in the freezer and freeze up to 6 months in fridge freezer or 12 months in a deep freezer. Thaw in the fridge overnight, or a bowl of warm water for about 20 minutes, before adding contents of bag plus 1 cup water to electric pressure cooker insert. You will skip the browning on Saute mode step when cooking from frozen. Pressure cook as directed.

If cooking freezer meal from partially thawed, add the hot water to the insert, add the frozen ingredients and adjust Pressure Cook time to 65 minutes.

Instant Pot Salmon with Lemon & Dill

Yield:	4 servings
Prep Time:	5 minutes
Cook Time:	2 minutes plus pressure build and release time

Ingredients

- 1 lb. salmon fillet, cut into 4 pieces
- 1 cup water
- Salt and pepper
- 1/4 cup + 3 tsp lemon juice, divided
- 3 tsp fresh dill, chopped
- Side: rice
- Side: veggies

Prepare to Freeze Instructions

- Chop the dill. Cut the salmon into smaller fillets.
- To gallon-size plastic freezer baggie in a round bowl/dish, add the following ingredients:
  - Salmon pieces
  - Salt and pepper
  - 1/4 cup lemon juice
  - 3 Tbsp chopped dill
  - Do NOT add water to the freezer meal bag, add that at time of pressure cooking
- Remove as much air as possible and seal. Add label to baggie and freeze.

Cooking Directions

1. Add 1 cup water plus 1/4 cup lemon juice to the electric pressure cooker insert. Add the steam rack.
2. Place the salmon pieces, skin side down, on the steam rack. Season with salt and pepper.
3. Drizzle 1 tsp lemon juice onto each salmon fillet. Sprinkle the fresh dill on top of each salmon fillet. Close the lid.
4. Steam valve: Sealing.
5. Cook on: Steam for 2 minutes.
6. Release: Natural.
7. Cook the rice and veggies.
8. Serve Instant Pot Salmon with Lemon & Dill with side of rice and veggies.

Freeze, Thaw & Pressure Cook Instructions

Put baggie in the freezer and freeze up to 6 months in fridge freezer or 12 months in a deep freezer. Thaw completely before adding 1 cup water to insert, then the salmon to steam rack in the electric pressure cooker insert. Pressure cook as directed.

Instant Pot Three Bean & Beef Chili

Yield: 4 servings
Prep Time: 10 minutes
Cook Time: 15 minutes plus pressure build and release time

Ingredients

- 1 lb. ground beef
- 1 Tbsp minced onion
- 1 tsp garlic powder
- 2 cups beef broth
- 15 oz. can red kidney beans
- 15 oz. can black beans
- 15 oz. can pinto beans
- 15 oz. can diced tomatoes
- 6 oz. can tomato paste
- 2 Tbsp chili powder
- Salt and pepper to taste
- Shredded cheddar cheese, as garnish
- Crackers or loaf bread, as side dish

Prepare to Freeze Instructions

- Open and drain cans of red kidney beans, black beans, pinto beans, and diced tomatoes. Open the tomato paste.
- Brown the ground beef with minced onion and garlic powder in skillet. Drain, if needed.
- To gallon-size plastic freezer baggie in a round bowl/dish, add the following ingredients:
  - Browned ground beef
  - 15 oz. can red kidney beans
  - 15 oz. can black beans
  - 15 oz. can pinto beans
  - 15 oz. can diced tomatoes
  - 6 oz. can tomato paste
  - 2 Tbsp chili powder
  - Do NOT add beef broth to the freezer meal bag, add that at time of pressure cooking
- Remove as much air as possible and seal. Add label to baggie and freeze.

Cooking Directions

1. Open and drain cans of red kidney beans, black beans, pinto beans, and diced tomatoes. Open the tomato paste.
2. In a large skillet, brown the ground beef with the minced onion and garlic powder. Drain and add the browned ground beef to the pressure cooker insert.
3. Note: You can skip the skillet and brown the ground beef using the Saute Mode of your Instant Pot. Tap on Saute, adjust to More/High, and brown the ground beef with the minced onion and garlic powder. Drain, if needed, and return the browned ground beef to the insert.
4. Stir in the black beans, tomato sauce, chili powder, salt and pepper with the hot water into the electric pressure cooker insert.
5. Steam valve: Sealing.
6. Cook on: Manual/High for 15 minutes, or use Beans/Chili pre-set function.
7. Release: Natural or Quick.
8. Serve Instant Pot Three Bean & Beef Chili with shredded cheese garnish, and crackers or loaf bread.

Freeze, Thaw & Pressure Cook Instructions

Put baggie in the freezer and freeze up to 6 months in fridge freezer or 12 months in a deep freezer. Thaw in the fridge overnight, or a bowl of warm water for about 20 minutes, before adding contents of bag plus 2 cups beef broth to electric pressure cooker insert. Pressure cook as directed.

If cooking freezer meal from partially thawed, add the hot water to the insert, add the frozen ingredients and adjust Pressure Cook time to 30 to 35 minutes.

Week #1
Meal Plan & Shopping List

Instant Pot 5-Ingredient Chili

Instant Pot Asian Shredded Beef

Instant Pot Cheesy Garlic Pork Chops

Instant Pot Green Chile Chicken Street Tacos

Instant Pot Ranchero Chicken

Note: The following meal plans are written with 5 recipes that double to make a total of 10 meals. The shopping lists and instructions are written to make 2 meals worth of each recipe.

1. Instant Pot 5-Ingredient Chili

Yield: *4 servings*
Active Time: *10 minutes. Cook Time: 30 minutes*

Recipe is written to make a single meal. Assembly Prep Directions & Shopping Lists will both contain directions and ingredients to make 2 meals, based on the number of servings you selected.

** This ingredient is used on the day you cook this meal. It is not added at the time you assemble and prepare your meals for the freezer.

Ingredients for Single Meal

- 1 - lb(s) ground beef
- 1 - small white onion(s)
- 2 - 15 oz. can(s) red kidney beans
- 2 - 15 oz diced tom & green chile
- 2 - Tbsp chili powder
- - Salt and pepper
- Garnish: - shredded cheese**
- 1 - cup(s) hot water**
- Side: - salad**
- 1 - gallon-size freezer baggie(s)

Cooking Directions for Single Meal

1. Dice the onion.
2. Open and drain the 2 cans of red kidney beans. Open 2 cans diced tomatoes with green chiles.
3. In a large skillet, brown the ground beef with the onion and some salt and pepper. Drain and add the browned ground beef to the pressure cooker insert.
4. Mix in the diced tomatoes with green chiles, drained red kidney beans, chili powder and hot water into the electric pressure cooker insert.
5. Steam valve: Sealing.
6. Pressure Cook: Manual/High for 15 minutes.
7. Release: Natural or Quick.
8. Prepare the salad.
9. Serve Instant Pot 5-Ingredient Chili with shredded cheese garnish and salad.

Assembly Prep Directions for 2 Meals

- Brown 2 lbs. ground beef.
- Dice onions.

- Open and drain 4 cans of red kidney beans.
- Open 4 cans of diced tomatoes with green chiles.
- To each gallon-size plastic freezer baggie in a round bowl/dish, add the following ingredients:
  - Half of the browned ground beef
  - Half of the drained red kidney beans
  - Half of the diced tomatoes with green chiles
  - Half of the diced onion
  - 2 Tbsp chili powder
  - Salt and pepper
- Remove as much air as possible and seal. Add label to baggie and freeze.

Freeze & Thaw Instructions: *Put baggie in the freezer and freeze up to 6 months in fridge freezer or 12 months in a deep freezer. Thaw in the fridge overnight, or a warm bowl of water for about 20 minutes, before transferring to pressure cooker insert with hot water and pressure cooking.*

Special Notes: *See myfreezeasy.com/ pressurecooker for more tips and tricks. Add 5-10 minutes of pressure cooking time, if cooking from completely frozen or partially frozen. Note that preheat time and release time may vary by appliance.*

Dairy-Free Modifications: *Omit cheese garnish for dairyfree meal.*

Gluten-Free Modifications: *Recipe is gluten-free when served with gluten-free sides.*

2. Instant Pot Asian Shredded Beef

Yield: 4 servings
Active Time: 10 minutes. Cook Time: 45 minutes

Recipe is written to make a single meal. Assembly Prep Directions & Shopping Lists will both contain directions and ingredients to make 2 meals, based on the number of servings you selected.

** This ingredient is used on the day you cook this meal. It is not added at the time you assemble and prepare your meals for the freezer.

Ingredients for Single Meal

- 2 - lb(s) beef chuck roast
- 1/2 - cup(s) hot water**
- - Salt and pepper
- 1/3 - cup(s) hoisin sauce
- 1/3 - cup(s) soy sauce
- 2 - Tbsp rice vinegar
- 2 - Tbsp honey
- 1 - Tbsp sesame oil
- 1 - tsp ground ginger
- 1 - tsp crushed red pepper
- Garnish: - sliced green onions**
- Side: - rice**
- Side: - veggies**
- 1 - gallon-size freezer baggie(s)

Cooking Directions for Single Meal

1. Place the beef roast into the base of the electric pressure cooker insert with the hot water and season with salt and pepper.
2. In a mixing bowl, whisk together the hoisin sauce, soy sauce, rice vinegar, honey, sesame oil, ginger and crushed red pepper.
3. Pour the sauce over the beef in the electric pressure cooker insert.
4. Steam value: Sealing.
5. Cook on: Manual/High for 45 minutes.
6. Release: Natural or Quick.
7. Once finished cooking, shred the beef with 2 forks and mix into the sauce.
8. Cook the rice, as directed.
9. Prepare the veggies.
10. Serve Instant Pot Asian Shredded Beef over rice with veggies and green onion garnish.

Assembly Prep Directions for 2 Meals

- In a mixing bowl, whisk together 2/3 cup hoisin sauce, 2/3 cup soy sauce, 4 Tbsp rice vinegar, 4 Tbsp honey, 2 Tbsp sesame oil, 2 tsp ground ginger and 2 tsp crushed red pepper.
- To each gallon-size plastic freezer baggie in a round bowl/dish, add the following ingredients:
  - 2 lb. beef chuck roast
  - Salt and pepper
  - Half of the prepared sauce
- Remove as much air as possible and seal. Add label to baggie and freeze.

Freeze & Thaw Instructions: *Put baggie in the freezer and freeze up to 6 months in fridge freezer or 12 months in a deep freezer. Thaw in the fridge overnight, or a warm bowl of water for about 20 minutes, before transferring to pressure cooker insert with hot water. Pressure cook as directed.*

Special Notes: *Add 5-10 minutes of pressure cooking time, if cooking from completely frozen or partially frozen. Note that preheat time and release time may vary by appliance. See myfreezeasy.com/EPC for more tips and tricks.*

Dairy-Free Modifications: *Recipe is dairy-free when served with dairy-free sides.*

Gluten-Free Modifications: *Recipe is gluten-free when you make it with gluten-free soy sauce and hoisin sauce.*

3. Instant Pot Cheesy Garlic Pork Chops

Yield: 4 servings
Active Time: 5 minutes. Cook Time: 35 minutes

Recipe is written to make a single meal. Assembly Prep Directions & Shopping Lists will both contain directions and ingredients to make 2 meals, based on the number of servings you selected.

** This ingredient is used on the day you cook this meal. It is not added at the time you assemble and prepare your meals for the freezer.

Ingredients for Single Meal

- 4 - boneless pork chops
- 1/2 - cup(s) hot water**
- - Salt and pepper
- 2 - Tbsp melted butter
- 2 - tsp minced garlic
- 1 - tsp onion powder
- 1 - cup(s) shredded mild cheddar cheese**
- Side: - dinner rolls**
- Side: - veggies**
- 1 - gallon-size freezer baggie(s)

Cooking Directions for Single Meal

1. Place the pork chops into the electric pressure cooker insert and season with salt and pepper. Add the hot water.
2. In a small bowl, stir the melted butter, minced garlic, and onion powder. Brush it onto the pork chops.
3. Steam Valve: Sealing
4. Cook on: Manual/High for 20 minutes.
5. Release: Natural or Quick.
6. Once lid is opened, leave on warm and add a few pinchfuls of shredded mild cheddar cheese onto each pork chop. Let sit for 3 to 5 minutes for cheese to melt.
7. Prepare veggies.
8. Warm the dinner rolls.
9. Serve Instant Pot Cheesy Garlic Pork Chops with veggies and dinner rolls.

Assembly Prep Directions for 2 Meals

- In a small bowl, stir 4 Tbsp melted butter, 4 tsp minced garlic, and 2 tsp onion powder.
- To each gallon-size plastic freezer baggie in a round bowl/dish, add the following ingredients:
  - 4 boneless pork chops
  - Melted butter mixture, brushed onto each pork chop
- Remove air from bag, add label and freeze.

Freeze & Thaw Instructions: *Put baggie in the freezer and freeze up to 6 months in fridge freezer or 12 months in a deep freezer. Thaw in the fridge overnight, or a warm bowl of water for about 20 minutes, before transferring to pressure cooker insert with hot water. Pressure cook as directed and top with shredded cheese after cooking.*

Special Notes: *Add 5-10 minutes of pressure cooking time, if cooking from completely frozen or partially frozen. Note that preheat time and release time may vary by appliance. See myfreezeasy.com/EPC for more tips and tricks.*

Dairy-Free Modifications: *Unfortunately, there isn't a great dairy-free option for this meal.*

Gluten-Free Modifications: *Recipe is gluten-free when served with gluten-free sides.*

4. Instant Pot Green Chile Chicken Street Tacos

Yield: 4 servings
Active Time: 10 minutes. Cook Time: 30 minutes

Recipe is written to make a single meal. Assembly Prep Directions & Shopping Lists will both contain directions and ingredients to make 2 meals, based on the number of servings you selected.

** This ingredient is used on the day you cook this meal. It is not added at the time you assemble and prepare your meals for the freezer.

Ingredients for Single Meal

- 2 - large boneless chicken breasts
- 4 - boneless chicken thighs
- 1/2 - cup(s) hot water**
- 1 - cup(s) green salsa
- 1 - 4 oz. can(s) green chiles
- 1 - Tbsp ground cumin
- - Salt and pepper
- 12 - corn tortillas**
- Garnish: - sour cream**
- Garnish: - chopped cilantro**
- Side: - veggies**
- 1 - gallon-size freezer baggie(s)

Cooking Directions for Single Meal

1. Open the green chiles.
2. Place the chicken breasts and chicken thighs into the electric pressure cooker insert with the hot water. Add the green salsa, green chilies, ground cumin, salt and pepper on top of the chicken.
3. Steam valve: Sealing.
4. Cook on: Manual/High for 15 minutes.
5. Release: Natural or Quick.
6. Once finished cooking, shred the chicken with 2 forks and mix into the green chile sauce.
7. Spoon the shredded chicken into corn tortillas.
8. Prepare veggies.
9. Serve Instant Pot Green Chile Chicken Street Tacos with sour cream and cilantro garnish with veggies.

Assembly Prep Directions for 2 Meals

- Open 2 cans of green chilies.
- To each gallon-size plastic freezer baggie in a round bowl/dish, add the following ingredients:
  - 2 large boneless chicken breasts
  - 4 boneless chicken thighs
  - 1 cup green salsa
  - 4 oz. can green chiles
  - 1 Tbsp ground cumin
  - Salt and pepper
- Remove as much air as possible and seal. Add label to baggie and freeze.

Freeze & Thaw Instructions: *Put baggie in the freezer and freeze up to 6 months in fridge freezer or 12 months in a deep freezer. Thaw in the fridge overnight, or a warm bowl of water for about 20 minutes, before adding contents of bag plus water to electric pressure cooker insert. Pressure cook as directed.*

Special Notes: *See myfreezeasy.com/EPC for more tips and tricks. Add 5-10 minutes of pressure cooking time, if cooking from completely frozen or mostly frozen. Note that preheat time and release time may vary by appliance.*

Dairy-Free Modifications: *Recipe is dairy-free when omit the sour cream garnish.*

Gluten-Free Modifications: *Recipe is gluten-free when served with gluten-free sides.*

5. Instant Pot Ranchero Chicken

Yield: 4 servings
Active Time: 10 minutes. Cook Time: 30 minutes

Recipe is written to make a single meal. Assembly Prep Directions & Shopping Lists will both contain directions and ingredients to make 2 meals, based on the number of servings you selected.

** This ingredient is used on the day you cook this meal. It is not added at the time you assemble and prepare your meals for the freezer.

Ingredients for Single Meal

- 1 - 15 oz. can(s) diced tomatoes
- 1 - 6 oz. can(s) tomato paste
- 3 - Tbsp taco seasoning
- 1/2 - lb(s) boneless chicken breasts
- 1/2 - cup(s) hot water**
- 1/2 - lb(s) boneless chicken thighs
- - Salt and pepper
- Side: - rice**
- Side: - veggies**
- 1 - gallon-size freezer baggie(s)

Cooking Directions for Single Meal

1. Whisk together the diced tomatoes with their juices and the tomato paste in the electric pressure cooker insert. Stir in the taco seasoning.
2. Add the chicken breast, thighs, and the hot water to the sauce in the electric pressure cooker insert. Spoon the sauce over the top.
3. Steam valve: Sealing.
4. Cook on: Manual/High for 15 minutes.
5. Release: Natural or Quick.
6. Once cooked, pull apart the chicken with 2 forks.
7. Cook rice, as directed.
8. Prepare veggies.
9. Serve Instant Pot Ranchero Chicken over rice with side of veggies.

Assembly Prep Directions for 2 Meals

- Open 2 cans of diced tomatoes.
- Open 2 cans of tomato paste.
- To each gallon-size plastic freezer baggie in a round bowl/dish, add the following ingredients:
  - Half of the canned diced tomatoes
  - Half of the canned tomato paste
  - 3 Tbsp taco seasoning
  - 1/2 lb. boneless chicken breasts
  - 1/2 lb. boneless chicken thighs
  - Salt and pepper
- Remove as much air as possible and seal. Add label to baggie and freeze.

Freeze & Thaw Instructions: *Put baggie in the freezer and freeze up to 6 months in fridge freezer or 12 months in a deep freezer. Thaw in the fridge overnight, or a warm bowl of water for about 20 minutes, before adding contents of bag plus water to electric pressure cooker insert. Pressure cook as directed.*

Special Notes: *See myfreezeasy.com/EPC for more tips and tricks. Add 5-10 minutes of pressure cooking time, if cooking from completely frozen or mostly frozen. Note that preheat time and release time may vary by appliance.*

Dairy-Free Modifications: *Recipe is dairy-free when served with dairy-free sides.*

Gluten-Free Modifications: *Recipe is gluten-free when served with gluten-free sides.*

Complete Shopping List by Recipe

1. Instant Pot 5-Ingredient Chili

- ☐ 2 - lb(s) ground beef
- ☐ 2 - small white onion(s)
- ☐ 4 - 15 oz. can(s) red kidney beans
- ☐ 4 - 15 oz. can(s) diced tom & green chile
- ☐ 4 - Tbsp chili powder
- ☐ - Salt and pepper
- ☐ - shredded cheese
- ☐ 2 - cup(s) hot water
- ☐ - salad
- ☐ 2 - gallon-size freezer baggie(s)

2. Instant Pot Asian Shredded Beef

- ☐ 4 - lb(s) beef chuck roast
- ☐ 1 - cup(s) hot water
- ☐ - Salt and pepper
- ☐ 2/3 - cup(s) hoisin sauce
- ☐ 2/3 - cup(s) soy sauce
- ☐ 4 - Tbsp rice vinegar
- ☐ 4 - Tbsp honey
- ☐ 2 - Tbsp sesame oil
- ☐ 2 - tsp ground ginger
- ☐ 2 - tsp crushed red pepper
- ☐ - sliced green onions
- ☐ - rice
- ☐ - veggies
- ☐ 2 - gallon-size freezer baggie(s)

3. Instant Pot Cheesy Garlic Pork Chops

- ☐ 8 - boneless pork chops
- ☐ 1 - cup(s) hot water
- ☐ - Salt and pepper
- ☐ 4 - Tbsp melted butter
- ☐ 4 - tsp minced garlic
- ☐ 2 - tsp onion powder
- ☐ 2 - cup(s) shredded mild cheddar cheese
- ☐ - dinner rolls
- ☐ - veggies
- ☐ 2 - gallon-size freezer baggie(s)

4. Instant Pot Green Chile Chicken Street Tacos

- ☐ 4 - large boneless chicken breasts
- ☐ 8 - boneless chicken thighs
- ☐ 1 - cup(s) hot water
- ☐ 2 - cup(s) green salsa
- ☐ 2 - 4 oz. can(s) green chiles
- ☐ 2 - Tbsp ground cumin
- ☐ - Salt and pepper
- ☐ 24 - corn tortillas
- ☐ - sour cream
- ☐ - chopped cilantro
- ☐ - veggies
- ☐ 2 - gallon-size freezer baggie(s)

5. Instant Pot Ranchero Chicken

- ☐ 2 - 15 oz. can(s) diced tomatoes
- ☐ 2 - 6 oz. can(s) tomato paste
- ☐ 6 - Tbsp taco seasoning
- ☐ 1 - lb(s) boneless chicken breasts
- ☐ 1 - cup(s) hot water
- ☐ 1 - lb(s) boneless chicken thighs
- ☐ - Salt and pepper
- ☐ - rice
- ☐ - veggies
- ☐ 2 - gallon-size freezer baggie(s)

Complete Shopping List by Store Section/Category

Meat

- ☐ 2 lb(s) ground beef
- ☐ 4 lb(s) beef chuck roast
- ☐ 8 boneless pork chops
- ☐ 4 large boneless chicken breasts
- ☐ 8 boneless chicken thighs
- ☐ 1 lb(s) boneless chicken breasts
- ☐ 1 lb(s) boneless chicken thighs

Produce

- ☐ 2 small white onion(s)
- ☐ **Side:** salad
- ☐ **Garnish:** sliced green onions
- ☐ **Side:** veggies
- ☐ **Garnish:** chopped cilantro

Pantry Staples - Canned, Boxed

- ☐ 4 - 15 oz. can(s) red kidney beans
- ☐ 4 - 15 oz. can(s) diced tom & green chile
- ☐ **Side:** rice
- ☐ 2 cup(s) green salsa
- ☐ 2 - 4 oz. can(s) green chiles
- ☐ 2 - 15 oz. can(s) diced tomatoes
- ☐ 2 - 6 oz. can(s) tomato paste

Starchy Sides

- ☐ **Side:** dinner rolls
- ☐ 24 corn tortillas

Sauces/Condiments

- ☐ 2/3 cup(s) hoisin sauce
- ☐ 2/3 cup(s) soy sauce
- ☐ 4 Tbsp rice vinegar
- ☐ 4 Tbsp honey
- ☐ 2 Tbsp sesame oil

Spices

- ☐ 4 Tbsp chili powder
- ☐ Salt and pepper
- ☐ 2 tsp ground ginger
- ☐ 2 tsp crushed red pepper
- ☐ 4 tsp minced garlic
- ☐ 2 tsp onion powder
- ☐ 2 Tbsp ground cumin
- ☐ 6 Tbsp taco seasoning

Dairy/Frozen

- ☐ **Side:** shredded cheese
- ☐ 2 cup(s) shredded mild cheddar cheese
- ☐ **Garnish:** sour cream

Supplies

- ☐ 6 cup(s) hot water
- ☐ **Side:** 10 gallon-size freezer baggie(s)
- ☐ 4 Tbsp melted butter

Freezer Meal Prep Day Shopping List by Recipe

Note: This shopping list doesn't include any side dish items like rice, dinner rolls, veggies or salad.
**In addition to a shopping list for prep day, this list could be used to help you organize ingredients on your counter before you begin preparing the meals for the freezer.

1. Instant Pot 5-Ingredient Chili

- ☐ 2 lb(s) ground beef
- ☐ 2 small white onion(s)
- ☐ 4 - 15 oz. can(s) red kidney beans
- ☐ 4 - 15 oz. can(s) diced tom & green chile
- ☐ 4 Tbsp chili powder
- ☐ Salt and pepper
- ☐ 2 gallon-size freezer baggie(s)

2. Instant Pot Asian Shredded Beef

- ☐ 4 lb(s) beef chuck roast
- ☐ Salt and pepper
- ☐ 2/3 cup(s) hoisin sauce
- ☐ 2/3 cup(s) soy sauce
- ☐ 4 Tbsp rice vinegar
- ☐ 4 Tbsp honey
- ☐ 2 Tbsp sesame oil
- ☐ 2 tsp ground ginger
- ☐ 2 tsp crushed red pepper
- ☐ 2 gallon-size freezer baggie(s)

3. Instant Pot Cheesy Garlic Pork Chops

- ☐ 8 boneless pork chops
- ☐ Salt and pepper
- ☐ 4 Tbsp melted butter
- ☐ 4 tsp minced garlic
- ☐ 2 tsp onion powder
- ☐ 2 gallon-size freezer baggie(s)

4. Instant Pot Green Chile Chicken Street Tacos

- ☐ 4 large boneless chicken breasts
- ☐ 8 boneless chicken thighs
- ☐ 2 cup(s) green salsa
- ☐ 2 - 4 oz. can(s) green chiles
- ☐ 2 Tbsp ground cumin
- ☐ Salt and pepper
- ☐ 2 gallon-size freezer baggie(s)

5. Instant Pot Ranchero Chicken

- ☐ 2 - 15 oz. can(s) diced tomatoes
- ☐ 2 - 6 oz. can(s) tomato paste
- ☐ 6 Tbsp taco seasoning
- ☐ 1 lb(s) boneless chicken breasts
- ☐ 1 lb(s) boneless chicken thighs
- ☐ Salt and pepper
- ☐ 2 gallon-size freezer baggie(s)

Freezer Meal Prep Day Shopping List by Store Section/Category

Note: *This shopping list doesn't include any side dish items like fruit, dinner rolls, veggies or salad.*

Meat

- ☐ 2 lb(s) ground beef
- ☐ 4 lb(s) beef chuck roast
- ☐ 8 boneless pork chops
- ☐ 4 large boneless chicken breasts
- ☐ 8 boneless chicken thighs
- ☐ 1 lb(s) boneless chicken breasts
- ☐ 1 lb(s) boneless chicken thighs

Produce

- ☐ 2 small white onion(s)

Pantry Staples - Canned, Boxed

- ☐ 4 - 15 oz. can(s) red kidney beans
- ☐ 4 - 15 oz. can(s) diced tom & green chile
- ☐ 2 cup(s) green salsa
- ☐ 2 - 4 oz. can(s) green chiles
- ☐ 2 - 15 oz. can(s) diced tomatoes
- ☐ 2 - 6 oz. can(s) tomato paste

Sauces/Condiments

- ☐ 2/3 cup(s) hoisin sauce
- ☐ 2/3 cup(s) soy sauce
- ☐ 4 Tbsp rice vinegar
- ☐ 4 Tbsp honey
- ☐ 2 Tbsp sesame oil

Spices

- ☐ 4 Tbsp chili powder
- ☐ Salt and pepper
- ☐ 2 tsp ground ginger
- ☐ 2 tsp crushed red pepper
- ☐ 4 tsp minced garlic
- ☐ 2 tsp onion powder
- ☐ 2 Tbsp ground cumin
- ☐ 6 Tbsp taco seasoning

Supplies

- ☐ 10x gallon-size freezer baggie(s)
- ☐ 4 Tbsp melted butter

Meal Assembly Instructions

- ☐ Label your bags/foil with printable labels or sharpie.
- ☐ Pull out all the ingredients into a central location or into stations.

Pre-Cook & Chop Instructions

- ☐ Brown 2 lbs. ground beef.
- ☐ Dice onions.
- ☐ In a small bowl, stir 4 Tbsp melted butter, 4 tsp minced garlic, and 2 tsp onion powder.
- ☐ In a mixing bowl, whisk together 2/3 cup hoisin sauce, 2/3 cup soy sauce, 4 Tbsp rice vinegar, 4 Tbsp honey, 2 Tbsp sesame oil, 2 tsp ground ginger and 2 tsp crushed red pepper.
- ☐ Open and drain 4 cans of red kidney beans.
- ☐ Open 4 cans of diced tomatoes with green chiles.
- ☐ Open 2 cans of green chilies.
- ☐ Open 2 cans of diced tomatoes.
- ☐ Open 2 cans of tomato paste.

The Assembly Prep should take between 30 to 35 minutes.

Assembly by Recipe (Set Out on the Counter)

If you prefer to load your freezer baggies and trays one recipe at a time, you can follow the below instructions.

Instant Pot 5-Ingredient Chili

To each gallon-size plastic freezer baggie in a round bowl/dish, add the following ingredients:

- Half of the browned ground beef
- Half of the drained red kidney beans
- Half of the diced tomatoes with green chiles
- Half of the diced onion
- 2 Tbsp chili powder
- Salt and pepper

Remove as much air as possible and seal. Add label to baggie and freeze.

Instant Pot Asian Shredded Beef

To each gallon-size plastic freezer baggie in a round owl/dish, add the following ingredients:

- 2 lb. beef chuck roast
- Salt and pepper
- Half of the prepared sauce

Remove as much air as possible and seal. Add label to baggie and freeze.

Instant Pot Cheesy Garlic Pork Chops

To each gallon-size plastic freezer baggie in a round bowl/dish, add the following ingredients:

- 4 boneless pork chops
- Melted butter mixture, brushed onto each pork chop

Remove as much air as possible and seal. Add label to baggie and freeze.

Instant Pot Green Chile Chicken Street Tacos

To each gallon-size plastic freezer baggie in a round bowl/dish, add the following ingredients:

- 2 large boneless chicken breasts
- 4 boneless chicken thighs
- 1 cup green salsa
- 4 oz. can green chiles
- 1 Tbsp ground cumin
- Salt and pepper

Remove as much air as possible and seal. Add label to baggie and freeze.

Instant Pot Ranchero Chicken

To each gallon-size plastic freezer baggie in a round bowl/dish, add the following ingredients:

- Half of the canned diced tomatoes
- Half of the canned tomato paste
- 3 Tbsp taco seasoning
- 1/2 lb. boneless chicken breasts
- 1/2 lb. boneless chicken thighs
- Salt and pepper

Remove as much air as possible and seal. Add label to baggie and freeze.

Week #2
Meal Plan & Shopping List

Instant Pot Butter Chicken

Instant Pot Herbed Pork Tenderloin

Instant Pot Lemon & Dill Salmon

Instant Pot One-Pot Spaghetti

Instant Pot Taco Soup

Note: The following meal plans are written with 5 recipes that double to make a total of 10 meals. The shopping lists and instructions are written to make 2 meals worth of each recipe.

1. Instant Pot Butter Chicken

Yield: 4 servings
Active Time: 10 minutes. Cook Time: 40 minutes

Recipe is written to make a single meal. Assembly Prep Directions & Shopping Lists will both contain directions and ingredients to make 2 meals, based on the number of servings you selected.

** This ingredient is used on the day you cook this meal. It is not added at the time you assemble and prepare your meals for the freezer.

Ingredients for Single Meal

- 2 - large boneless chicken breasts
- 4 - boneless chicken thighs
- 1/2 - cup(s) hot water**
- 1/4 - cup(s) butter
- 1 - small white onion(s)
- 1 - 8 oz can(s) tomato sauce
- 2 - tsp minced garlic
- 1 - Tbsp garam masala
- 1 - cup(s) chicken stock
- - Salt and pepper
- 1 - cup(s) heavy cream**
- Side: - pita bread**
- Side: - salad**
- 1 - gallon-size freezer baggie(s)

Cooking Directions for Single Meal

1. Dice the onion.
2. Place the chicken breasts and chicken thighs into the electric pressure cooker insert with the hot water. Add the butter, diced white onions, tomato sauce, minced garlic, garam masala, chicken stock, salt and pepper on top of the chicken.
3. Steam valve: Sealing.
4. Cook on: Manual/High for 15 minutes.
5. Release: Natural or Quick.
6. After you open the lid, stir in the heavy cream and keep on warm setting for 5 minutes to heat through.
7. Once finished cooking, gently shred the chicken with 2 forks and mix into the sauce.
8. Prepare the salad.
9. Serve Instant Pot Butter Chicken with pita bread and salad.

Assembly Prep Directions for 2 Meals

- Dice 2 onions.
- Open 2 cans of tomato sauce.
- To each gallon-size plastic freezer baggie in a round bowl/dish, add the following ingredients:
  - 2 large boneless chicken breasts
  - 4 boneless chicken thighs
  - 1/4 cup butter
  - Half of the diced onion
  - Half of the tomato sauce
  - 2 tsp minced garlic
  - 1 Tbsp garam masala
  - 1 cup chicken stock
- Remove as much air as possible and seal. Add label to baggie and freeze.

Freeze & Thaw Instructions: *Put baggie in the freezer and freeze up to 6 months in fridge freezer or 12 months in a deep freezer. Thaw in the fridge overnight, or a warm bowl of water for about 20 minutes, before adding contents of bag plus water to electric pressure cooker insert. Pressure cook as directed. After cooking, stir in heavy cream and keep on warm setting for 5 minutes to warm through.*

Special Notes: *See myfreezeasy.com/EPC for more tips and tricks. Add 5-10 minutes of pressure cooking time, if cooking from completely frozen or mostly frozen. Note that preheat time and release time may vary by appliance.*

Dairy-Free Modifications: *Make with dairy-free margarine and stir in 1 cup canned coconut milk in place of the cream.*

Gluten-Free Modifications: *Recipe is gluten-free if served over rice.*

2. Instant Pot Herbed Pork Tenderloin

Yield: 4 servings
Active Time: 10 minutes. Cook Time: 40 minutes

Recipe is written to make a single meal. Assembly Prep Directions & Shopping Lists will both contain directions and ingredients to make 2 meals, based on the number of servings you selected.

** This ingredient is used on the day you cook this meal. It is not added at the time you assemble and prepare your meals for the freezer.

Ingredients for Single Meal

- 2 - lb(s) pork tenderloin
- 1/2 - cup(s) hot water**
- - Salt and pepper
- 1 - Tbsp minced onion
- 1 - tsp minced garlic
- 1 - tsp dried oregano
- 1 - tsp dried basil
- 1 - tsp dried rosemary
- Side: - veggies**
- Side: - dinner rolls**
- 1 - gallon-size freezer baggie(s)

Cooking Directions for Single Meal

1. Place the pork roast into the electric pressure cooker insert with the hot water. Season with salt and pepper.
2. In a small bowl, toss together the minced onion, minced garlic, dried oregano, dried basil and dried rosemary. Add the herb mixture directly onto the pork roast, pressing lightly.
3. Steam valve: Sealing.
4. Cook on: Manual/High for 40 minutes.
5. Release: Natural or Quick.
6. Once finished cooking, slice the pork roast. Season with salt and pepper to taste.
7. Prepare veggies.
8. Warm the dinner rolls.
9. Serve Instant Pot Herb Pork Tenderloin with veggies and dinner rolls.

Assembly Prep Directions for 2 Meals

- In a small bowl, toss together 2 Tbsp minced onion, 2 tsp minced garlic, 2 tsp dried oregano, 2 tsp dried basil, and 2 tsp dried rosemary.
- To each gallon-size plastic freezer baggie in a round bowl/dish, add the following ingredients:
  - 2 lb. pork tenderloin
  - Salt and pepper
  - Half of the herb mixture
- Remove as much air as possible and seal. Add label to baggie and freeze.

Freeze & Thaw Instructions: *Put baggie in the freezer and freeze up to 6 months in fridge freezer or 12 months in a deep freezer. Thaw in the fridge overnight, or a warm bowl of water for about 20 minutes, before adding contents of bag plus water to electric pressure cooker insert. Pressure cook as directed.*

Special Notes: *See myfreezeasy.com/EPC for more tips and tricks.*
Add 5-10 minutes of pressure cooking time, if cooking from completely frozen or mostly frozen. Note that preheat time and release time may vary by appliance.

Dairy-Free Modifications: *Recipe is dairy-free when served with dairy-free sides.*

Gluten-Free Modifications: *Recipe is gluten-free when served with gluten-free sides, like rice or mashed potatoes.*

3. Instant Pot Lemon & Dill Salmon

Yield: 4 servings
Active Time: 10 minutes. Cook Time: 2 minutes

Recipe is written to make a single meal. Assembly Prep Directions & Shopping Lists will both contain directions and ingredients to make 2 meals, based on the number of servings you selected.

** This ingredient is used on the day you cook this meal. It is not added at the time you assemble and prepare your meals for the freezer.

Ingredients for Single Meal

- 1 - lb(s) salmon fillet
- - Salt and pepper
- 2 - tsp lemon juice
- 2 - tsp fresh dill
- Side: - veggies**
- Side: - rice**
- 1 - gallon-size freezer baggie(s)

Cooking Directions for Single Meal

1. Add 1 cup of water to the electric pressure cooker insert and then add the steam rack.
2. Place the 4 salmon fillets flat on the steam rack, skin side down. Sprinkle each with little salt and pepper over the top. Drizzle lemon juice over the salmon pieces. Place fresh chopped dill sprigs on salmon.
3. Steam valve: Sealing.
4. Cook on: Manual/High for 2 minutes.
5. Release: Natural or Quick.
6. Cook rice as directed on package.
7. Prepare veggies, as needed.
8. Once salmon is cooked, carefully lift it out of the electric pressure cooker insert onto a shallow serving dish. Remove skin and serve.
9. Serve Instant Pot Lemon & Dill Salmon with rice and veggies.

Assembly Prep Directions for 2 Meals

- Cut 2 lbs. salmon into 8 - 1/4 lb. fillets.
- Halve 4 lemons.
- Finely chop 4 tsp fresh dill.
- To each gallon-size plastic freezer baggie in a round bowl/dish, add the following ingredients:
  - Half of the salmon fillets
  - Salt and pepper
  - Juice from 2 lemons
  - Half of the chopped dill
- Remove as much air as possible and seal. Add label to baggie and freeze.

Freeze & Thaw Instructions: *Put baggie in the freezer and freeze up to 6 months in fridge freezer or 12 months in a deep freezer. Thaw in the fridge overnight, or a warm bowl of water for about 20 minutes, before transferring to the electric pressure cooker and cooking as directed.*

Dairy-Free Modifications: *Recipe is dairy-free when served with dairy-free sides.*

Gluten-Free Modifications: *Recipe is gluten-free when served with gluten-free sides.*

4. Instant Pot One-Pot Spaghetti

Yield: 4 servings
Active Time: 15 minutes. Cook Time: 6 plus pressure build and release time update

Recipe is written to make a single meal. Assembly Prep Directions & Shopping Lists will both contain directions and ingredients to make 2 meals, based on the number of servings you selected.

** This ingredient is used on the day you cook this meal. It is not added at the time you assemble and prepare your meals for the freezer.

Ingredients for Single Meal

- 1 - lb(s) ground beef
- 1 - Tbsp minced onion
- 1 - tsp garlic powder
- 1 - 26 oz. jar(s) marinara sauce
- 16 - oz. spaghetti noodles
- 2 1/2 - cup(s) beef stock
- Garnish: - Parmesan cheese
- Side: - salad
- 1 - gallon-size freezer baggie(s)

Cooking Directions for Single Meal

1. Add the ground beef, minced onion, and garlic powder to the electric pressure cooker insert. Set on Saute mode and brown the ground beef in the insert. Once browned, stir in the marinara sauce.
2. Break the noodles in half or thirds and mix into the sauce and then pour the beef stock over the top. Give it a gentle stir and then press all the noodles into the liquid.
3. Close the lid, set to sealing.
4. Set on Manual, High Pressue and cook for 6 minutes.
5. Let naturally release for 5 minutes, then finish the release by setting to Venting.
6. The sauce will look too thin, but give it a stir and it will thicken up with the pasta and meat.
7. Serve Instant Pot One-Pot Spaghetti with Parmesan cheese garnish, and a side salad.

Assembly Prep Directions for 2 Meals

- Brown 1 lb ground beef with 1 Tbsp minced onion and 1 tsp garlic powder.
- Brown 1/2 lb ground beef with 1/2 Tbsp minced onion and 1/2 tsp garlic powder.
- Brown 1 1/2 lbs ground beef with 1 1/2 Tbsp minced onion and 1 1/2 tsp garlic powder.
- Brown 2 lbs ground beef with 2 Tbsp minced onion and 2 tsp garlic powder.
- To each gallon-size plastic freezer baggie in a round bowl/dish, add the following ingredients:
  ○ Ground beef, browned and cooled
  ○ 1 - 26 oz. jar marinara sauce
  ○ Salt and pepper
  ○ Do NOT add beef stock or pasta the freezer meal bag, add that at time of pressure cooking
- Remove as much air as you can and seal. Freeze up to 6 months in your fridge freezer or 12 months in a deep freezer.

Freeze & Thaw Instructions: *Put baggie in the freezer and freeze up to 6 months in fridge freezer or 12 months in a deep freezer. Thaw completely. Transfer to pressure cooker, then pressure cook as directed with pasta and 2 1/2 cups beef stock, chicken stock or water.*

5. Instant Pot Taco Soup

Yield: 4 servings
Active Time: 15 minutes. Cook Time: 25 minutes

Recipe is written to make a single meal. Assembly Prep Directions & Shopping Lists will both contain directions and ingredients to make 2 meals, based on the number of servings you selected.

** This ingredient is used on the day you cook this meal. It is not added at the time you assemble and prepare your meals for the freezer.

Ingredients for Single Meal

- 1 - lb(s) ground beef
- 1 - 15 oz. can(s) black beans
- 1 - 15 oz. can(s) diced tomatoes
- 1 - 15 oz. can(s) corn
- 2 - Tbsp chili powder
- 1 - tsp ground cumin
- 1 - tsp garlic powder
- 1 - tsp onion powder
- - Salt and pepper
- Garnish: - corn tortilla chips**
- Garnish: - shredded cheese**
- Side: - veggies**
- 2 - cup(s) chicken broth
- 1 - cup(s) hot water**
- 1 - gallon-size freezer baggie(s)

Cooking Directions for Single Meal

1. In a large saucepan, brown and drain the ground beef. Drain and add the browned ground beef to the pressure cooker insert.
2. Add the black beans, corn, diced tomatoes, and chicken broth into the electric pressure cooker insert.
3. Stir in the chili powder, ground cumin, garlic powder, onion powder and hot water in with the other ingredients.
4. Steam valve: Sealing.
5. Cook on: Manual/High for 15 minutes.
6. Release: Natural or Quick.
7. Serve Instant Pot Taco Soup, with crushed tortilla chips and cheese as garnish, with a side of veggies.

Assembly Prep Directions for 2 Meals

- Brown and drain 2 lbs. ground beef.
- Open, drain and rinse 2 cans of black beans.
- Open 2 cans of diced tomatoes.
- Open and drain 2 cans of corn.
- To each gallon-size plastic freezer baggie in a round bowl/dish, add the following ingredients:
    - Half of the browned ground beef into each bag
    - 15 oz. can black beans, drained and rinsed
    - 15 oz. can diced tomatoes, undrained
    - 15 oz. can corn, drained
    - 2 Tbsp chili powder
    - 1 tsp ground cumin
    - 1 tsp garlic powder
    - 1 tsp onion powder
    - 2 cups chicken broth or equivalent bouillon base plus water
- Remove as much air as possible and seal. Add label to baggie and freeze.

Freeze & Thaw Instructions: *Put baggie in the freezer and freeze up to 6 months in fridge freezer or 12 months in a deep freezer. Thaw in the fridge overnight, or a warm bowl of water for about 20 minutes, before transferring to pressure cooker insert with hot water.*

Special Notes: *Add 5-10 minutes of pressure cooking time, if cooking from completely frozen or partially frozen. Note that preheat time and release time may vary by appliance. See myfreezeasy.com/EPC for more tips and tricks.*

Dairy-Free Modifications: *Omit cheese as garnish.*

Gluten-Free Modifications: *Recipe is gluten-free when served with gluten-free sides.*

Complete Shopping List by Recipe

1. Instant Pot Butter Chicken

- ☐ 4 - large boneless chicken breasts
- ☐ 8 - boneless chicken thighs
- ☐ 1 - cup(s) hot water
- ☐ 1/2 - cup(s) butter
- ☐ 2 - small white onion(s)
- ☐ 2 - 8 oz. can(s) tomato sauce
- ☐ 4 - tsp minced garlic
- ☐ 2 - Tbsp garam masala
- ☐ 2 - cup(s) chicken stock
- ☐ - Salt and pepper
- ☐ 2 - cup(s) heavy cream
- ☐ - pita bread
- ☐ - salad
- ☐ 2 - gallon-size freezer baggie(s)

2. Instant Pot Herbed Pork Tenderloin

- ☐ 4 - lb(s) pork tenderloin
- ☐ 1 - cup(s) hot water
- ☐ - Salt and pepper
- ☐ 2 - Tbsp minced onion
- ☐ 2 - tsp minced garlic
- ☐ 2 - tsp dried oregano
- ☐ 2 - tsp dried basil
- ☐ 2 - tsp dried rosemary
- ☐ - veggies
- ☐ - dinner rolls
- ☐ 2 - gallon-size freezer baggie(s)

3. Instant Pot Lemon & Dill Salmon

- ☐ 2 - lb(s) salmon fillet
- ☐ - Salt and pepper
- ☐ 4 - tsp lemon juice
- ☐ 4 - tsp fresh dill
- ☐ - veggies
- ☐ - rice
- ☐ 2 - gallon-size freezer baggie(s)

4. Instant Pot One-Pot Spaghetti

- ☐ 2 - lb(s) ground beef
- ☐ 2 - Tbsp minced onion
- ☐ 2 - tsp garlic powder
- ☐ 2 - 26 oz. jar(s) marinara sauce
- ☐ 2 - 16 oz. spaghetti noodles
- ☐ 5 - cup(s) beef stock
- ☐ - Parmesan cheese
- ☐ - salad
- ☐ 2 - gallon-size freezer baggie(s)

5. Instant Pot Taco Soup

- ☐ 2 - lb(s) ground beef
- ☐ 2 - 15 oz. can(s) black beans
- ☐ 2 - 15 oz. can(s) diced tomatoes
- ☐ 2 - 15 oz. can(s) corn
- ☐ 4 - Tbsp chili powder
- ☐ 2 - tsp ground cumin
- ☐ 2 - tsp garlic powder
- ☐ 2 - tsp onion powder
- ☐ - Salt and pepper
- ☐ - corn tortilla chips
- ☐ - shredded cheese
- ☐ - veggies
- ☐ 4 - cup(s) chicken broth
- ☐ 2 - cup(s) hot water
- ☐ 2 - gallon-size freezer baggie(s)

Complete Shopping List by Store Section/Category

Meat

- ☐ 4 large boneless chicken breasts
- ☐ 8 boneless chicken thighs
- ☐ 4 lb(s) pork tenderloin
- ☐ 2 lb(s) salmon fillet
- ☐ 4 lb(s) ground beef

Produce

- ☐ 2 small white onion(s)
- ☐ **Side:** salad
- ☐ **Side:** veggies
- ☐ 4 tsp lemon juice
- ☐ 4 tsp fresh dill

Pantry Staples - Canned, Boxed

- ☐ 2 - 8 oz. can(s) tomato sauce
- ☐ 2 cup(s) chicken stock
- ☐ **Side:** rice
- ☐ 2 - 16 oz. spaghetti noodles
- ☐ 5 cup(s) beef stock
- ☐ 2 - 15 oz. can(s) black beans
- ☐ 2 - 15 oz. can(s) diced tomatoes
- ☐ 2 - 15 oz. can(s) corn
- ☐ 4 cup(s) chicken broth

Starchy Sides

- ☐ **Side:** pita bread
- ☐ **Side:** dinner rolls
- ☐ **Side:** corn tortilla chips

Sauces/Condiments

- ☐ 2 - 26 oz. jar(s) marinara sauce

Spices

- ☐ 6 tsp minced garlic
- ☐ 2 Tbsp garam masala
- ☐ Salt and pepper
- ☐ 4 Tbsp minced onion
- ☐ 2 tsp dried oregano
- ☐ 2 tsp dried basil
- ☐ 2 tsp dried rosemary
- ☐ 4 tsp garlic powder
- ☐ 4 Tbsp chili powder
- ☐ 2 tsp ground cumin
- ☐ 2 tsp onion powder

Dairy/Frozen

- ☐ 1/2 cup(s) butter
- ☐ 2 cup(s) heavy cream
- ☐ **Side:** Parmesan cheese
- ☐ **Side:** shredded cheese

Supplies

- ☐ 4 cup(s) hot water
- ☐ **Side:** 10 gallon-size freezer baggie(s)

Freezer Meal Prep Day Shopping List by Recipe

__Note:__ This shopping list doesn't include any side dish items like rice, dinner rolls, veggies or salad.
*__**__In addition to a shopping list for prep day, this list could be used to help you organize ingredients on your counter before you begin preparing the meals for the freezer.*

1. Instant Pot Butter Chicken

- ☐ 4 large boneless chicken breasts
- ☐ 8 boneless chicken thighs
- ☐ 1/2 cup(s) butter
- ☐ 2 small white onion(s)
- ☐ 2 - 8 oz. can(s) tomato sauce
- ☐ 4 tsp minced garlic
- ☐ 2 Tbsp garam masala
- ☐ 2 cup(s) chicken stock
- ☐ Salt and pepper
- ☐ 2 gallon-size freezer baggie(s)

2. Instant Pot Herbed Pork Tenderloin

- ☐ 4 lb(s) pork tenderloin
- ☐ Salt and pepper
- ☐ 2 Tbsp minced onion
- ☐ 2 tsp minced garlic
- ☐ 2 tsp dried oregano
- ☐ 2 tsp dried basil
- ☐ 2 tsp dried rosemary
- ☐ 2 gallon-size freezer baggie(s)

3. Instant Pot Lemon & Dill Salmon

- ☐ 2 lb(s) salmon fillet
- ☐ Salt and pepper
- ☐ 4 tsp lemon juice
- ☐ 4 tsp fresh dill
- ☐ 2 gallon-size freezer baggie(s)

4. Instant Pot One-Pot Spaghetti

- ☐ 2 lb(s) ground beef
- ☐ 2 Tbsp minced onion
- ☐ 2 tsp garlic powder
- ☐ 2 - 26 oz. jar(s) marinara sauce
- ☐ 2 - 16 oz. spaghetti noodles
- ☐ 5 cup(s) beef stock
- ☐ 2 gallon-size freezer baggie(s)

5. Instant Pot Taco Soup

- ☐ 2 lb(s) ground beef
- ☐ 2 - 15 oz. can(s) black beans
- ☐ 2 - 15 oz. can(s) diced tomatoes
- ☐ 2 - 15 oz. can(s) corn
- ☐ 4 Tbsp chili powder
- ☐ 2 tsp ground cumin
- ☐ 2 tsp garlic powder
- ☐ 2 tsp onion powder
- ☐ Salt and pepper
- ☐ 4 cup(s) chicken broth
- ☐ 2 gallon-size freezer baggie(s)

Freezer Meal Prep Day Shopping List by Store Section/Category

Note: *This shopping list doesn't include any side dish items like fruit, dinner rolls, veggies or salad.*

Meat

- ☐ 4 large boneless chicken breasts
- ☐ 8 boneless chicken thighs
- ☐ 4 lb(s) pork tenderloin
- ☐ 2 lb(s) salmon fillet
- ☐ 4 lb(s) ground beef

Produce

- ☐ 2 small white onion(s)
- ☐ 4 tsp lemon juice
- ☐ 4 tsp fresh dill
- ☐ salad

Pantry Staples - Canned, Boxed

- ☐ 2 - 8 oz. can(s) tomato sauce
- ☐ 2 cup(s) chicken stock
- ☐ 2 - 16 oz. spaghetti noodles
- ☐ 5 cup(s) beef stock
- ☐ 2 - 15 oz. can(s) black beans
- ☐ 2 - 15 oz. can(s) diced tomatoes
- ☐ 2 - 15 oz. can(s) corn
- ☐ 4 cup(s) chicken broth

Sauces/Condiments

- ☐ 2 - 26 oz. jar(s) marinara sauce

Spices

- ☐ 6 tsp minced garlic
- ☐ 2 Tbsp garam masala
- ☐ Salt and pepper
- ☐ 4 Tbsp minced onion
- ☐ 2 tsp dried oregano
- ☐ 2 tsp dried basil
- ☐ 2 tsp dried rosemary
- ☐ 4 tsp garlic powder
- ☐ 4 Tbsp chili powder
- ☐ 2 tsp ground cumin
- ☐ 2 tsp onion powder

Dairy/Frozen

- ☐ 1/2 cup(s) butter
- ☐ Parmesan cheese

Supplies

- ☐ 10x gallon-size freezer baggie(s)

Meal Assembly Instructions

- ☐ Label your bags/foil with printable labels or sharpie.
- ☐ Pull out all the ingredients into a central location or into stations.

Pre-Cook & Chop Instructions

- ☐ Brown and drain 2 lbs. ground beef.
- ☐ Brown 1 lb ground beef with 1 Tbsp minced onion and 1 tsp garlic powder.
- ☐ Brown 1/2 lb ground beef with 1/2 Tbsp minced onion and 1/2 tsp garlic powder.
- ☐ Brown 1 1/2 lbs ground beef with 1 1/2 Tbsp minced onion and 1 1/2 tsp garlic powder.
- ☐ Brown 2 lbs ground beef with 2 Tbsp minced onion and 2 tsp garlic powder.
- ☐ Cut 2 lbs. salmon into 8 - 1/4 lb. fillets.
- ☐ Halve 4 lemons.
- ☐ Finely chop 4 tsp fresh dill.
- ☐ Dice 2 onions.
- ☐ In a small bowl, toss together 2 Tbsp minced onion, 2 tsp minced garlic, 2 tsp dried oregano, 2 tsp dried basil, and 2 tsp dried rosemary.
- ☐ Open, drain and rinse 2 cans of black beans.
- ☐ Open 2 cans of diced tomatoes.
- ☐ Open and drain 2 cans of corn.
- ☐ Open 2 cans of tomato sauce.

The Assembly Prep should take between 30 to 35 minutes.

Assembly by Recipe (Set Out on the Counter)

If you prefer to load your freezer baggies and trays one recipe at a time, you can follow the below instructions.

Instant Pot Butter Chicken

To each gallon-size plastic freezer baggie in a round bowl/dish, add the following ingredients:

- 2 large boneless chicken breasts
- 4 boneless chicken thighs
- 1/4 cup butter
- Half of the diced onion
- Half of the tomato sauce
- 2 tsp minced garlic
- 1 Tbsp garam masala
- 1 cup chicken stock

Remove as much air as possible and seal. Add label to baggie and freeze.

Instant Pot Herbed Pork Tenderloin

To each gallon-size plastic freezer baggie in a round bowl/dish, add the following ingredients:

- 2 lb. pork tenderloin
- Salt and pepper
- Half of the herb mixture

Remove as much air as possible and seal. Add label to baggie and freeze.

Instant Pot Lemon & Dill Salmon

To each gallon-size plastic freezer baggie in a round bowl/dish, add the following ingredients:

- Half of the salmon fillets
- Salt and pepper
- Juice from 2 lemons
- Half of the chopped dill

Remove as much air as possible and seal. Add label to baggie and freeze.

Instant Pot One-Pot Spaghetti

To each gallon-size plastic freezer baggie in a round bowl/dish, add the following ingredients:

- Ground beef, browned and cooled
- 1 - 26 oz. jar marinara sauce
- Salt and pepper
- Do NOT add beef stock or pasta the freezer meal
- bag, add that at time of pressure cooking

Remove as much air as you can and seal. Freeze up to 6 months in your fridge freezer or 12 months in a deep freezer.

Instant Pot Taco Soup

To each gallon-size plastic freezer baggie in a round bowl/dish, add the following ingredients:

- Half of the browned ground beef into each bag
- 15 oz. can black beans, drained and rinsed
- 15 oz. can diced tomatoes, undrained
- 15 oz. can corn, drained
- 2 Tbsp chili powder
- 1 tsp ground cumin
- 1 tsp garlic powder
- 1 tsp onion powder
- 2 cups chicken broth or equivalent bouillon base plus water

Remove as much air as possible and seal. Add label to baggie and freeze.

Get More Freezer Meal Plans Like These!

MyFreezEasy allows you to create the perfect freezer meal plan, made up of recipes that you choose and that your family will love. Freezer meals save money on groceries, time in the kitchen and some stress at the dinner hour too.

Load up your freezer with make-ahead meals and dinnertime will be a breeze!

Don't forget to sign up for the free MyFreezEasy online workshop, you'll learn just about everything you need to know about freezer cooking and how it can transform your family's dinner experience.

Sign up for free at: www.myfreezeasy.com/workshop

FREE
Freezer Cooking
Online Workshop

GET STARTED

Made in the USA
Middletown, DE
15 September 2018